ST. MARY'S COLLEGE OF MARYLAND
ST. MARY'S CITY, MARYLAND

Perspectives of a Moroccan Nationalist

Perspectives
of a Moroccan
NATIONALIST

DOUGLAS E. ASHFORD
CORNELL UNIVERSITY

The Bedminster Press

*Readers of this book are invited to send
name and address to The Bedminster Press,
Vreeland Avenue, Totowa, New Jersey, U.S.A.,
to receive announcements and literature about
other books in the social sciences
published by The Bedminster Press.*

Contents

PREFACE

I Introduction to the Moroccan Survey 1

II Span and Stress of Occupational Differences 15

III Divergence and Discontinuity in Education 31

IV Submersion of Linguistic Distinctions 47

V Nation-Building and Confidence in Office 61

VI Religious Decompression in Political Life 73

VII Removing the Aftermath of Violence 87

VIII Diminishing Returns of Nationalist Unity 101

IX Opposition Threat—Real or Imagined? 113

X The Social Roots of Consensus 125

XI From Nationalism to Nationhood 137

APPENDIX I: Questionnaire 155

APPENDIX II: Questionnaire Administration 167

Tables

I-1　Provincial Composition of Samples by Percentages　7

I-2　Educational Composition of Samples by Percentages　8

I-3　Linguistic Skills of Samples by Percentages　9

I-4　Occupational Composition of Samples by Percentages　10

I-5　Age Composition of Samples by Percentages　10

II-1　Provincial Distribution and Occupation by Percentages　17

II-2　Number of Memberships and Occupation by Percentages　19

II-3　Education and Occupation by Percentages　20

II-4　Age and Occupation by Percentages　21

II-5　Date of Organization and Occupation by Percentages　22

II-6　Date of Recruitment and Occupation by Percentages　24

III-1　Provincial Distribution and Education by Percentages　33

III-2　Number of Memberships and Education by Percentages　34

III-3　Age and Education by Percentages　38

III-4　Date of Attaining Office and Education by Percentages　40

III-5　Date of Recruitment and Education by Percentages　41

IV-1　Provincial Distribution and Language by Percentages　50

IV-2　Memberships and Language by Percetnages　51

IV-3　Occupation and Language by Percentages　53

IV-4   Date of Recruitment and Languages by Percentages   56

IV-5   Estimates of Preparation for Office and Language   59

V-1   Estimates of Preparation for Present and Higher Office   62

V-2   Estimates of Preparation, Aspiration, and Previous Office   64

V-3   Estimates of Preparation, Aspiration and Provincial Differences   65

V-4   Estimates of Preparation, Aspiration and Occupation   68

V-5   Estimates of Preparation, Aspiration and Age   70

VI-1   Education and Religious Self-Estimates by Percentages   80

VI-2   Age and Religious Self-Estimates by Percentages   81

VI-3   Previous Office and Religious Self-Estimates by Percentages   82

VII-1   Date of Recruitment and Resistance Participation by
          Percentages   91

VII-2   Membership and Resistance Participation by Percentages   93

VII-3   Education and Resistance Participation by Percentages   94

VII-4   Occupation and Resistance Participation by Percentages   96

VIII-1   Occupation and Unity Attitudes by Percentages   107

IX-1   Importance Given the Opposition   117

IX-2   Date of Recruitment and Opposition Attitude by Percentages   119

X-1   Social Differences and Issue Evaluation   130

Preface

The data for this inquiry were collected in mid-1958, when the author was working on a more general study of the Moroccan transition to independence. The opportunity to administer a questionnaire to the Istiqlal cadre arose quite unexpectedly, but was much too tempting to reject. The questionnaire was prepared quite quickly, and dealt with several problems of general concern as well as the immediate research objectives of the author. Several of the special problems raised in the survey were presented in articles in *World Politics*, the *American Political Science Review*, and the *Public Opinion Quarterly*. However, the author felt, partly because of the scarcity of comparable guidelines in designing his own questionnaire, that it would be useful to have a more inclusive account of the results. They may help some who are interested in applying survey techniques in the non-Western setting, and they may dissuade others from explorations of this kind. They certainly provide us with a much better description of a crucial, but little known, group of Moroccan nationalists.

In presenting the general results of the survey two closely related frames of reference will be used. The data enable us, first, to see how effective the party has been in placing its more talented officials and in meeting the rapidly increasing expectations and aspirations they attach to the nationalist movement. Secondly, the data provide some glimpses into the political psychology of the party militant in a new nation. Great caution must be exercised in generalizing from the data, and it is hoped that the repeated qualification of the data will remind the reader that the findings have no statistical significance beyond the actual sample. It is not likely that systematic sampling of the kind needed for studies of non-Western national characteristics will be possible for many years.

However, this does not mean that survey data from carefully selected, strategic groups cannot be of great help in understanding the politics of Africa and Asia.

Although the author would be the first to assert that the information used here must be combined with our general knowledge in order to have maximum value, there is a rather frightening chance of falling between two stools. The survey analyst of Western experience may be dissatisfied with the mechanical aspects of the inquiry and the relatively small sample. Although the size of the sample compares favorably with those used in other non-Western studies of this kind, there remain a myriad of problems of translation, administration, comprehension, and coding. All possible precautions were taken, as described in more detail below. The most drastic of these was to reduce the number of respondents mercilessly on the basis of their performance on some of the more complex questions. The discarded responses were nevertheless processed, and it was found that their more fragmentary responses generally confirmed the trends established with the small sample.

The second risk is meeting the expectations of the Orientalist. The most reassuring reply to the cultural specialist is that many of the problems analyzed below would otherwise be difficult, if not impossible, to study. Several of the questions involve areas of sensitivity, which were seldom discussed in the author's presence even by his close friends in Morocco. Even where sensitivity is not involved, it would still be physically most difficult to accumulate the body of information represented in the questionnaire returns. The results, then, are a useful addition to our description of the Arab world in a strictly conventional way as well as an exploration in the application of contemporary behavioral techniques to the problems of political development in a new nation.

In preparing this study, I have benefited greatly from the advice and encouragement of many persons. The questionnaire was administered during my first visit to Morocco in 1957-1958 which was made possible by the Ford Foundation. While in Morocco several Istiqlal officials supported the study, especially Mehdi Ben Barka, now a leader of the UNFP, and Mohammed Ben Chekroun, the Istiqlal's administrative secretary. While the questionnaire was being printed, Mr. Lahlou of *Al-Alam* was most cooperative, and Mohammed Lamrani helped decipher a variety of Arabic handwriting. The party also shared the printing costs with the author.

The preliminary exploration of the data took place at Indiana University, and was made possible by funds from the Graduate School. The author is indebted to many there for support, including Walter H. C. Laves, Charles S. Hyneman, Edward H. Buehrig, and P. J. Vatikiotis. Though they share no responsibility for the shortcomings of this inquiry, Milton Hobbs, Karl Schuessler, Kenneth Janda, Henry Teune and Frederick W. Frey supplied a stimulating variety of comments as the data processing advanced. The revision of the manuscript was made possible by a summer Research Fellowship from the Center of Middle East Studies at Harvard University, for which the author thanks Profs. H. A. R. Gibb and A. J. Meyer. I am particularly obliged to Cecil Asfour, who was my research assistant throughout preparation of the first draft. Secretarial work was diligently performed by Mrs. Phyllis Durnal in Bloomington, and by Misses Margaret Pacsu and Irene Van Duyn at Harvard. The manuscript's appearance was delayed when the author returned to North Africa in 1961-1962, but the study has hopefully benefited from the additional reflection and field work of the past two years, made possible by the Social Science Research Council.

Douglas E. Ashford

Washington, D. C.
June 1963

Perspectives of a Moroccan Nationalist

I

Introduction to the Moroccan Survey

In the not too distant past inquiry into the attitudes and opinions of a group as remote from American life as the North African nationalists would have provoked skepticism, if not bewilderment. Today, of course, many are familiar with American military interest (rapidly being withdrawn) in Morocco, the dynamic leadership of Bourguiba in Tunisia, and the bitter, tragic conflict in Algeria. Like their newly independent counterparts around the world the countries of the Maghreb have begun to control their own destinies. To do so has proved to be a more prolonged and more disillusioning task than the nationalists probably expected. Even with the irritating and sometimes self-defeating tactics of colonial powers discounted, the new governments have managed to survive the hazards of independence with only the barest margin of safety.

In both the Western and non-Western worlds, however one wishes to make this elusive distinction, we know little of how the rapid transition to independence relates to the views of the newly created citizens. In the midst of the uncertainty that confronts every newly established government stands the greatest uncertainty of all: how has the shock of independence combined with the experience of the nationalist struggle? The new leaders lack the reservoir of common understanding and practical skill that enable the experienced leader to evaluate the expectations of the followers. The aggressiveness and daring of much of the leadership in the developing countries may actually be a function of leaders' inability and therefore their refusal, to make such judgments. To behave moderately and to make effective plans one must be able to estimate the expectations of others.

1

Perspectives of a Moroccan Nationalist

One may not assume, however, that all uncertainty is concentrated in the higher echelons of responsibility simply because it is more readily observable at such levels. An uncertain leader with a decided people can often manage very nicely. A more profound problem appears to be the confusion, often mixed with the discouragement, of the people as a whole on the eve of independence. It is to this problem that the present inquiry is addressed, although the findings are both tentative and rudimentary. In a sense there are no fixed points of reference to guide the new political system. Popular indicators are few for many reasons. The people are not in the habit of expressing opinions even where they may possess the literary skill to do so with considerable sophistication. In the absence of the range of symbols, terms and procedures that are fashioned in older political systems, the new citizen, like the leader, may find moderation difficult to express. It is probably not too much of a distortion to assert that rational, compromising attiudes are as important an ingredient in the effective, viable political sysem as the nucleus of common value referred to as patriotic loyalty or simply nationalist fervor.

The present inquiry, then, will be concerned with the usefulness of certain indicators in understanding the local officials of the Moroccan nationalist movement, and in studying their political attitudes and background. In a strictly exploratory fashion it will also be concerned with what attitudes and characteristics seem to be associated with a limited number of defined problems, which are fairly common in the development of new countries. The concluding essay will attempt to summarize and integrate by comparing how the respondents have agreed or disagreed in various frames of reference. The study is admittedly exploratory and elementary, but in an area where there has been little exploration and where we generally lack elementary knowledge. There can be no claim to valid statistical generalization, although several devices of statistical description have been used.[1]

---

[1] This will come as no surprise to those who have worked with survey methods in non-Western countries. For example see Daniel Lerner, *The Passing of Traditional Society*, Glencoe, Free Press, 1958, and also Morroe Berger, *Bureaucracy and Society in Modern Egypt*, Princeton, Princeton University Press, 1957. Both these studies are based on samples that limit generalization, although the first deals with a general problem on a cross-cultural basis and the second with particular problems of one country. For a useful summary of the state of this kind of research in non-Western countries see the special issue of the *Public Opinion Quarterly*, v. 22, no. 3, (February 1958).

Although further justification is probably not required once these conditions are stated, the inquiry's purpose may be more nearly filled if some of the author's speculations on the state of research in the developing areas are briefly noted. The formulation of complex hypotheses presupposes the existence of a body of general knowledge where the student may seek key relationships and find operational definitions for the key terms of his hypotheses. It is probably fair to state that the social sciences are just arriving at this degree of sophistication. To establish suitable hypotheses for solving some of the problems of the developing areas some elementary ground-breaking is needed. From this may emerge either lines of theoretical speculation particularly suited to the non-West or, more likely, avenues for comparison between the West and non-West. Much imaginative study of our own society is of limited value in non-Western inquiry because we do not yet know how to attach appropriate significance to the more common social variables in the new setting. While it is absurd to select indicators, characteristics and relationships at random, there are also certain advantages to be drawn from presenting findings on widely used characteristics in simple form.

A second and related concern is the extent to which our failure to explore the commonplace contributes to the preservation of clichés, ambiguities and misleading conclusions. Lines of comparability and more general theoretical schemes must be found on demonstrable grounds unless one wishes to cast aside empirical inquiry and rely solely on intuition. Political science, and especially the politics of the unfamiliar countries, probably has more than its proportionate share of untested and untestable generalizations. It is certainly hoped that the present inquiry will bring the attention of a variety of scholars to some of the fundamental relationships and problems of political studies in the non-West. In addition, it is hoped that the findings will underscore some useful formulations for subsequent empirical study of the more pressing problems of the non-West. Although the following analyses may lack the rigor used in studying comparable questions in the United States, it is important that we begin to study the non-West as systematically as possible and that we utilize all relevant data.

The inquiry is based on data collected by written, Arabic questionnaires that were circulated to local party secretaries of the Moroccan Istiqlal party.[2] The party's history begins in the late 1920's, although

---

[2] For general background on Morocco see Nevill Barbour, *A Survey of North West*

it did not have an effective organization until the post-war period. At first the organization extended only to the coastal cities and more advanced farming regions. When Morocco's King Mohammed Ben Youssef was forcefully exiled in 1953, the party was almost totally suppressed and a new terrorist organization was begun. By then the party and the King were engaged in a coordinated effort that reached to all but the most isolated parts of the country. Two years of terrorism and repression ended with the French conceding independence to Morocco and Tunisia in 1956 in hopes of keeping Algeria.

In evaluating the data it is important to remember that the Istiqlal's post-independence organization, from which the sample is drawn, represents an almost complete break with the past. For two years party leaders were in prison or scattered throughout the world. The internal fight for independence was taken up by a new group of persons, young, urban and working class. In 1956 the Istiqlal tried to incorporate the new, more specialized nationalist groups, which were represented by the Council of the Resistance, the Liberation Army, and the U.M.T. (*Union Marocaine du Travail*). At the time the questionnaire was administered, early 1958, this delicate task was still being carried out with some success, but there were signs of tension among party leaders. By the end of 1958 the tensions within the party had repercussions among the members and the Istiqlal split.

The Istiqlal has two historical features that make it a particularly attractive focus. First, the post-independence reconstruction has meant that the party lost the discipline and coherence that a continuous organization might have sustained. In the hectic, but exuberant, first months of independence the party tried to recapture its pre-eminence with mass enrollments and indiscriminate officer selection at lower levels. Secondly, the party was quite aware that the superior organizations and strong loyalties of the resistance and labor movement were formidable challenges. So long as the party pictured itself as the first among equals, which it certainly wished to become during the period of the survey, its views were more inclusive and more compromising than they might have been otherwse. These factors contribute to making the Istiqlal more

Africa (The Maghrib), London, Oxford University Press, 1959. A history of Moroccan political developments is found in Rom Landau, *Morocco: 1900-1955*, San Francisco, American Academy of Asian Studies, 1956, and a study of the transition to independence is found in the author's *Political Change in Morocco*, Princeton, Princeton University Press, 1961. The questionnaires were not used in the author's earlier book.

representative in both its opinions and its personnel than its pre-independence structure would suggest.

By 1958 the party had an organization of over 1200 party secretaries. They were organized in a centralized, well-defined hierarchy with regional party inspectors and an active party headquarters in Rabat. The party agreed to distribute the questionnaire through its regional inspectors.[3] Each local secretary was to receive the questionnaire and an envelope, in which he was instructed to seal his reply. He also received received a letter from party headquarters.[4] The letter explained the questionnaire as an attempt to help the party as a whole in its national role and reassured the secretary that his response would be kept anonymous. He was also told that the sealing procedure was intended to make certain that the inspector, his immediate superior, did not see the reply. The total return was 337 questionnaires or about one-fourth of the secretaries.

There were, of course, immeasurable factors of illiteracy, disinterest and suspicion. Although the discipline of the party and the secretaries' interest in communications from Rabat probably contributed to the reliability of replies, there is no way to estimate distortion except by internal checks in the questionnaire itself and by the consistency of certain answers. Morocco is no exception among the many new countries lacking current, reliable statistical studies that might be utilized in evaluating the samples. For these reasons the student is almost entirely dependent on his own judgment in accepting and ruling out replies. The most important standard used here was performance on the series of fifteen, five-part preference questions. Any person having more than five omissions and/or partial responses to these questions was rejected.[5] This

---

[3] Since the inspector has considerable authority, a system of direct collection would have been preferable. However, the only terms on which the party would permit the survey were through its own communication system. Their caution is an interesting vestige of the colonial era, when no official communication channel was considered safe. For background on the inspectors see *Political Change in Morocco, op. cit., pp.* 232-243.

[4] The letter and the questionnaire are reprinted in Appendix I.

[5] The only acceptable partial response was an indication of only first and second choice, in which cases the remaining choices were coded as fourth choices to maintain a constant total score. Where entire questions were blank they were coded as entirely third choices for the same reason. Of the total of 93 responses for 15 questions (1395 completed preference questions) there were 92 blank or partial responses (66 blank and 26 partial). Certain preference questions seemed to elicit

was thought to be a reasonably high standard of performance in terms of the level of understanding and interest that it implies. In this way the sample was reduced from 337 persons to 93 or about one-sixteenth of all party secretaries.

The reduction in the sample is necessary in order to utilize the preference questions. Using the smaller sample has resulted in a somewhat more advanced group of persons than given by the total response to the questionnaire. Nevertheless, it is still probably safe to claim that the sample is less advanced by most social criteria and less sophisticated politically than most groups that we have been able to study in such detail. As the following tables indicate, the entire sample contains a large percentage of traditionally-oriented persons as measured by region, education and language skill. The changes brought about in selecting the smaller sample of 93 have most likely worked to increase the sample's intellectual ability and general political knowledge. At the same time the sample retains a sizable proportion of less advanced, more isolated citizens.

Bearing in mind that there is no justification for generalization beyond the size of the sample, it is possible to specify quite carefully the major characteristics of the eliminated responses. The regional shift is the most noticeable. The total sample was almost equally divided between provinces that are generally regarded as less advanced and more advanced. One must rely on direct observation in making such classifications in most new countries. The regions classified as more advanced commonly use modern agricultural techniques and have been largely assimilated into the modern commercial structure of the country. Tribal patterns of behavior have virtually disappeared and the people are within easy traveling distance of major cities. Forming the small sample on the basis of responses to the opinion questions has shifted the regional distribution toward the more advanced provinces. Although it is unfortunate to sacrifice representation of the more retarded provinces, of which we know much less, it is possible that many of the respondents in the retarded provinces were not able to understand parts of the question-

---

more omissions and errors, particularly those asking the secretary to give the choices he felt the members or population in his area of operation would make. These two questions, numbers 5 and 6, account for over-one-third of the errors and omissions (34), and are only used in Chapter X, which deals with the pattern of preferences, not their content.

naire. The increase in advanced provincial representation very likely works to increase the reliability of the responses.

The less advanced provinces are represented by Marrakech, Ouarzazate, Midelt and southern Rabat. The more advanced provinces are Meknes, Casablanca, Oujda and a scattering of responses from Fes and Agadir[6]. There were generally very few responses from many of the areas where the Istiqlal has a long organizational history. Some regional bias may have been introduced by the sponsorship of the questionnaire, which was most strongly supported by new, more progressive leaders. They were less highly regarded and possibly even suspected in the areas where an older, more traditional party bureaucracy was still in power.[7] Conversely, in the more advanced regions the new party organization had been built largely since independence under the supervision of the young leaders. There were also some indications that the elder party officials were less efficient and more suspicious of innovation of any kind.

Table I-1
PROVINCIAL COMPOSITION OF SAMPLES BY PERCENTAGES

	Discarded Groups Per Cent (N=244)	Analysis Group Per Cent (N=93)
Advanced	40	69
Retarded	60	31

As might be expected, educational and linguistic achievement increased noticeably in the smaller sample. However the proportionate importance of those in from the elementary or traditional Koranic schools (*musiid*) remained the same when the small sample was taken. The incomplete replies from many persons with elementary education are probably explained by the fact that many years are normally spent in the Koranic school where little else is taught except classical Arabic. The re-

---

6 Those familiar with Morocco might question including Agadir and Oujda among the more advanced provinces. An inspection of the responses shows that the secretaries are from more developed regions of the provinces, the Sous valley in the case of Agadir and the northeastern corner of Oujda. Marrakech has been classified as retarded despite the advanced agricultural economy that exists in some parts of it. The province was effectively isolated by the French Protectoratee through its puppet, Al Glaoui, and so was not exposed to systematic political activity until 1956.

7 A detailed analysis of the Istiqlal's organization will be found in the author's book, *op. cit.*, pp. 219-259, and also in a comparative article, "Transitional Politics in Morocco and Tunisia," *Current Problems in North Africa*, Princeton, Princeton University Conference Series, 1960, pp. 14-35.

spondents have, thus, developed considerable linguistic knowledge and little else. Nearly a third of the respondents had spent over eleven years in village Koranic schools. Working with the small sample no doubt seriously distorts the educational characteristics of the country, but it is still possible to make some suggestions on the vital question of education's role in a country undergoing rapid political change. Secondary schools are either government-operated institutions, mostly technical or trade schools, or party schools, generally known as "free schools" among Moroccans. Interesting in itself is the fact that there were no representatives of European universities in the entire sample. The university-educated are from Qarawiyn University in Fes or Moulay Youssef University in Marrakech, the two Muslim universities of Morocco.

Table I-2

EDUCATION COMPOSITION OF SAMPLES BY PERCENTAGES

	Discarded Group Per Cent (N=159)	Analysis Group Per Cent (N=79)
Elementary	76	54
Secondary	22	30
University	1	16

Morocco has a major language differentiation, which will also be studied in greater detail in one of the following essays. As the Islamic invasion of North Africa took place the Berber tribesmen were driven into the mountains, where their language survived in spoken form. Although the process of modernization is slowly creating a homogeneous setting in which Maghrebi Arabic is used, the language difference still exists in many parts of the country and Berber is still the sole language in a few areas.[8] A knowledge of Berber does not necessarily indicate that a person has all the orientations of the most remote Berber community, but only that he comes from a Berber-speaking region or that his affairs have taken him into such regions. There is, of course, a large transitional area

---

[8] There are, in fact, three major Berber dialects, which have not been differentiated here. One is found in the Rif Mountain area, another in the Middle Atlas Mountains and the third in the Sour Valley of Agadir. For the student new to Arab studies, a note on the Arabic language may also be helpful. Arabic has one written form which is generally spoken in a standard way by all scholars and called "classical" Arabic. The various Arabic-speaking regions of the world have developed their own usages and pronunciations, which accounts for the dialects. The Moroccan dialect is Maghrebi or western Arabic.

around tribal strongholds where Berber is used by elders or in more intimate communication and Arabic is used for business and formal communication.

One of the interesting indications that the sample has not lost all of its national significance and represents considerable rural opinion is denoted by the large percentage knowing a Berber dialect in both the discarded and analysis groups. However, the analysis group has a greatly reduced proportion of party officials speaking only Maghrebi Arabic. Selecting the small sample has worked in favor of higher general education, as might be expected, and has also increased in the percentage knowing classical Arabic, although it is hardly a well-known language.

Table I-3

LINGUISTIC SKILLS OF SAMPLES BY PERCENTAGES

	Discarded Group Per Cent (N=216)	Analysis Group Per Cent (N=91)
Berber	37	33
Classical Arabic	10	20
Bilingual	18	36
Maghrebi Only	35	11

The occupational breakdown was the least affected by the decrease in the sample. The occupations classified as modern, which include minor officials, small merchants, artisans and modern teachers, are a slightly larger percentage in the small sample, but over a third of respondents have traditional occupations in both samples. The traditional pursuits represented are small farmer (*fellah*), traditional school teacher (*fqih*), unskilled workers and servants. The relative increase was among those in modern occupations and no responses were almost totally eliminated. The persons inserting "no" as their reply to the question on occupation raise the intriguing issue as to whether or not the Istiqlal has itself created an occupational category of minor party officials. The group seems too large to be without general significance. The party has been known to give small sums to its militants or to intercede on their behalf to get some sort of sinecure from the government. The possibility of the nationalist party becoming a device for social and political advancement should not be ruled out in any developing country and will be further explored. The possibility that the unoccupied represent unemployed cannot be excluded, of course, but there were remarkably few persons in the entire response who indicated unemployment.

Table I-4

OCCUPATIONAL COMPOSITION OF SAMPLES BY PERCENTAGES

	Discarded Group Per Cent (N=221)	*Analysis Group* Per Cent (N=91)
Modern	24	34
Traditional	43	36
Unoccupied	33	30

The age structure of the small sample has more youth and fewer elders than the discarded group. The change in composition is accounted for by the apparent reluctance or inability of a larger proportion of older party secretaries, and a proportionately similar increase in the younger secretaries' responses. To some extent this confirms the interpretation of bias toward more recently organized regions of the country, mentioned above, since older secretaries are also more likely to be found in areas that have been organized for longer periods.

Table I-5

AGE COMPOSITION OF SAMPLES BY PERCENTAGES

	Discarded Group Per Cent (N=220)	*Analysis Group* Per Cent (N=91)
30 years or less	20	31
31-40 years	42	41
41 years or more	38	28

Thus, the most pronounced shifts between the analysis and the discarded groups are in education, language and regional distribution. In the case of educational level, however, much of the increase in higher education comes from the reduction of the no response group rather than from a decrease in those having elementary education. Likewise in the case of language, the rise in skill is partly an over-all increase although classical Arabic increases more sharply. The geographical distribution is altered in the small sample to conform more nearly to the distribution of total party organization. Smaller shifts take place in the age and occupational structure of the small sample, where modern occupations and youth are more heavily represented than the total response, would suggest to be the case in the entire party. On the whole it is probably fair to summarize these changes as favoring the earlier recruit and more experienced party secretary. Since these persons will undoubtedly continue to fill key roles in Morocco's political development, their experience and opinions are of great importance in understanding Morocco's future.

In writing the questionnaire it was expected that the respondent's organizational experience would yield insights into how political values and attitudes were shaped locally. The Istiqlal is the first and, for many, the only political organization that the local officials have known. Eighty-five of the 93 respondents joined the party before 1956[9], the first full year of order and independence. In the pre-independence period the party had been a more demanding and totally embracing group than since independence. The powerful solidarities of the struggle for independence and the ruthless persecution of the colonial regime could be expected to forge value and opinions that would endure past the moment of independence and color the new citizens' views. On this hypothesis it was hoped to find correlations between organizational experience and opinions, and, thereby, to gain some knowledge of how nationalist militants are affected by their party activities and obligations.

Six kinds of organizational information were used in the present study,[10] most often to estimate the respondent's position in the party communication system. The number of visits from the party's regional inspector in the last six months is used as an indicator of how opinions vary with exposure to official views and personal contact with superiors in the party hierarchy. Similar implications can be drawn from the party secretary's organizational level, which is identified as section or sub-section (*fara or dayira*). Though not often used, the number of elections since organization has also been coded as a rough indicator of how opinions and attitudes might vary where there is some evidence of greater member participation. It also provides insight into how, if at all, the nationalist movement may serve as a training ground for increased individual participation in other political groups. The three remaining

---

[9] A minor point should be made on the date of independence. The country officially dates independence from the Franco-Moroccan Agreement of March 2, 1956. However, the King was permitted to return to his country in November, 1955, from which time political activity was virtually unrestricted.

[10] As the questionnaire in Appendix I reveals, a variety of other information on party organization was collected, and has been used in analyses of other problems. The responses to the battery of organizational questions provide an indicator of what type of questions are best handled in situations of this kind and may be of use to subsequent students.

pieces of organizational data are the dates of organization, of taking present office and of recruitment. These will be especially valuable in analyzing the respondent's self-evaluation of his preparation for office and his party aspirations. They are, of course, also valuable indicators of length and intensity of party indoctrination and experience.

The following essays fall easily into three groups. The first group consists of three analyses of the importance of selected demographic variables. Although dealing with rudimentary relationships in very simple terms, the essays explore facets of some time-honored clichés and provide suggestions for hypotheses having well-defined, empirical referents. The essay on occupational differentiation is probably the first time that so broad a range of occupational differentiation in a new country has been subject to analysis in the light of a common political experience. The conclusions focus on the possible impact of the party bureaucracy on the over-all development of a new nation, and on the party's use of occupational skills. The second essay deals with how education relates to the political experience and background of the party secretaries. Probably no other achievement is so universally respected and enthusiastically sought in a developing nation, although we have very fragmentary evidence of how it may affect political attitudes and opinions in these circumstances. The third essay is an analysis of how linguistic skills relate to the secretaries' views and accomplishments. Language differentiaion was manipulated by the colonial regime to take on almost racial significance, although Berbers and Arabs are thoroughly intermixed. From time to time the old arguments are quietly revived so that an impartial examination may serve to put some generally destructive and fruitless views to rest.

The second group of essays is based on three self-evaluations, plus a study of the relation of participation in violence to the secretaries' background and opinions. The secretaries were asked to evaluate their preparation for their present office and also for higher office. The results tell us something of how party officials in a newly independent country evaluate their own qualifications, strengths and weaknesses. The findings take on additional value when combined with a closely related evaluation, the secretaries' aspiration for higher office. We have only the most rudimentary notion of what kinds of persons constitute the politically ambitious in a rapidly developing political system. Political recruitment at the intermediate societal level, i.e., village leaders, may very likely become a crucial factor in the encouragement or discouragement of democratic forms of government. The second evaluation study concerns the respondent's religious behavior. While there is no doubt of the general importance of religion in all Muslim countries, our knowledge of its relation to individual political behavior is largely limited to investigation of differences among sects and denominations. Very little investigation has been done on how intensity of belief or devoutness may relate to political views and to other political and social characteristics.

The essay on violence is of particular interest for it sheds some light on a form of political behavior that we have seldom attempted to study systematically. The political development of Morocco and many other new states has, unfortunately, been accompanied with considerable bloodshed. This was by no means entirely the fault of the colonial regimes involved, though it should not be forgotten that the colonial peoples received their first training in highly organized violence and their respect for superior massive force from their tutors. The experience of the Moroccans has certainly had lasting psychological and sociological effects. On several occasions there have been threats of renewed terrorism in the cities and there have been several armed revolts stemming from tribal discontent. It would be almost impossible to conduct an investigation into the subject of violence without the support of an accredited organization like the Istiqlal, which makes the available data well worth further analysis.

The last group of essays is based on interpretations of the preference questions. Using certain choices stated in these questions, the secretaries have been divided into groups that give varying degrees of support to more general goals.[11] The use of persons who have stated a given preference for a particular position in two or more situations adds a degree of reliability to the attitudinal differentiation. For example, several preferences elicited the respondent's opinions on the promotion of repre-

---

11 Preference questions establish, of course, only the respondent's order of choice and not the intensity of conviction or desire that any particular choice may hold in his mind. Two choices, and even two entire questions, may actually rest so far apart in the respondent's mind that they are not justifiably included in the same selection of choice or battery of questions. Put slightly differently, a first choice does not mean in every case that the respondent has a similar desire or feels similar approval for the choice so ranked.

sentative forms of government. Those who repeatedly gave such reforms high preference have been distinguished from others stating less approval. An analysis has then been made of what demographic characteristics and other preferences appear to prevail among groups of persons who are attitudinally differentiated. One essay distinguishes the respondents according to their attitude toward opposition party activity. Another essay is based on the importance attached to the national unity theme. It is perhaps the most vague framework of any of those used, but is so frequently used in the politics of developing countries that it is important to establish more precisely the nature of its appeal.

The final essay tries to bring together the analyses of the previous essays. Although they deal with distinct problems and relationships, each grouping of party secretaries has provided another tabulation of preferences. As will be explained in more detail below, the preferences ask the respondent to put himself in different political frameworks, e.g., to rank his preferences in relation to the needs of the nation in the past and in future. The preferences thus provide an indication of the extent to which choices are repeated in the various frameworks as well as what particular preferences are made. Using the twelve groupings of the respondents, some of whose opinions have been discussed in the previous essays, a simple statistical device has been used to construct a synopsis of the degree of similar or different ranking of the choices in each framework. This, in turn, provides evidence of how differences in political judgment occur in relation to various goals. Do the respondents, for example, express more common preferences when discussing the nation or the party, the past or the future, members of the party or the population as a whole? From these findings more precise hypotheses on consensus formation may be formed than has been previously possible. The findings constitute one method of systematically examining how political consensus emerges in a new nation, and suggest a method for measuring the development of consensus across cultural lines.

II
Span and Stress of Occupational Differences

The Moroccan nationalist movement sprang from two distinct occupational groups. On the one hand was a group of French educated and higher westernized leaders, and on the other a group of traditional, religious officials (*ulema*). Thus, the first impulse for the Istiqlal came from persons enjoying high social status in their respective walks of life, but hardly representing a cross section of Morocco's occupational pattern. The growth of the nationalist movement is in some respect the history of the acquiring such a cross section of Moroccan occupations. For nearly two decades, until the late 1940's, the party's occupational composition was restricted to those held in high esteem. The foundation of nationalist solidarity may very possibly have rested as heavily on the ease of appealing to several highly regarded and relatively small occupational groups as on the unifying simplicity of the party's goal.

From the moment of independence the party encountered all the conflicting views, needs and priorities that occupational diversity can create. The Istiqlal faced one particularly serious organizational repercussion of broad occupational differences. The industrial workers were united in a single trade union, the U.M.T., which was established several months prior to independence and had a superior organizational cadre.[1] The split of the Istiqlal in early 1959 is in many respects the result of the inability of worker and elder nationalist to agree, although both practice

---

[1] For more information on the internal politics of the U.M.T. see the author's "Labor Politics in a New Nation," *Western Political Quarterly*, v. 13, no. 2, June 1960, pp. 312-331.

their peculiar form of nationalism. Since the two organizations were distinct, the sample of party secretaries does not include many industrial workers. Only six persons in the total sample identified themselves as unskilled laborers and only three in the small sample. No one identified himself as industrial laborer in the small sample, although there were twelve who indicated membership in the U.M.T. For these reasons the sample must be regarded as lacking worker representation, which follows from the regional breakdown discussed above. The very fact that this was very likely characteristic of the party's occupational structure as late as two years after independence makes the schism between the U.M.T. and the Istiqlal more understandable.

As noted in Table I-4 approximately thirty per cent of both the discarded and the analysis groups indicated that they had no occupation beyond their work for the party, for they did not indicate unemployment. How this segment of party officials supports themselves is not clear, but the fact that large numbers of secretaries were apparently engaged only in party activity merits further exploration. There are many possibilities as to how they sustain themselves, not the least of which being party intervention to secure special privileges or token employment.[2] Since these secretaries apparently devote full time to the Istiqlal, it is reasonable to look upon them as a particularly influential and very likely a particularly loyal group of party supporters. Since there is little evidence that the Istiqlal has been able or even tried to move trained officials to areas of special need[3], one would expect to find the fully committed secretaries in places where the party has a long history.

SOCIAL BACKGROUND AND OCCUPATION

The provincial distribution of occupations[4] supports this speculation

---

[2] In a country where industrial and commercial enterprises are particularly limited, the power to issue licenses, permits, and quotas is very important. Officials frequently admitted to the author that special considerations affected granting these privileges. In addition, there is a certain amount of direct subsidy through minor officials assigned to various political groups. They generally are left free to work with groups in which the government has an interest.

[3] The questionnaire asked the respondents if they had served their previous office in a different place. Only four persons in the small sample indicated that they had not had previous office in the place they were working. There was almost no evidence in the author's field interviews that secretaries had moved in response to party needs.

[4] It will be noted that the sample by occupation is only 91 persons. Two persons

concerning the unidentified occupational group and also fulfills expectations concerning the distribution of traditional occupations. The provincial distribution is similar for modern and traditional occupations, while the "full-time" secretaries are heavily concentrated in the more advanced provinces. Nearly all the unoccupied secretaries are from provinces where the party has been active for many years. The distribution of modern and traditional occupations might have been influenced by the poorer communications and lower educational levels in the countryside, where there are undoubtedly more traditionally occupied persons working for the party. Nevertheless, it is interesting that as large a proportion of modern occupations as shown are located in the retarded provinces. In the uncondensed tabulation they are fairly evenly scattered among all the retarded provinces represented in the sample, and so may have a maximum social impact in their regions. The traditional occupations, however, are concentrated in Ouarzazate province, which was practically untouched by nationalist activity before 1956.[5] This suggests that more recent organization has relied more heavily on generally less experienced and less advanced groups, which will be confirmed by later evidence.

Table II-1

PROVINCIAL DISTRIBUTION AND OCCUPATION BY PERCENTAGES

	Modern Per Cent (N=31)	Traditional Per Cent (N=43)	Unoccupied Per Cent (N=27)
Advanced	65	54	89
Retarded	35	46	11
Chi square = .02*			

* It should be remembered that the chi square has limited meaning because of the imperfect sample. It indicates the chances that the observed distribution might vary from the expected distribution given the number of responses available, and has no meaning for a large universe.

did not indicate their occupation and have been omitted from all tables in this chapter. Where no response is indicated, it refers to no responses in addition to these two persons. The provincial breakdown is discussed in footnote 5 of Chapter I.

[5] Ouarzazate province, like all the Moroccan provinces along the Sahara, was under military administration during most of the Protectorate. After independence the first governor was Addi ou Bihi, whose resistance to any political organization led to his removal.

The rural-urban distinction is most useful in estimating how many of the respondents work in villages. The urban category includes the two major cities that responded to the questionnaire, Casablanca and Marrakech, and cities of over 20,000 inhabitants. The urban sample is not proportionate to the influence that the more effective urban population has, but is roughly proportionate to the degree of urbanization in the country. The rural category consists, then, entirely of villages and small market towns, which may be something more than the collection of huts found in villages. As might be expected, the traditional occupations are nearly all found in villages, while the other two occupational groups predominate in the cities and large towns. The modern occupational group that was urbanized was scattered among all locations, but the unoccupied secretaries were most heavily concentrated in the large towns. Since large towns are the places where party needs would make a full-time party-supported secretary most useful and where sinecures could be found, the findings are consistent with previous speculation on the role of the unoccupied secretaries.

In a country with diverse social settings a useful indicator of an individual's general advancement is the groups to which he belongs. Both the small number of widely organized groups and the ease of estimating their societal impact makes them attractive indices of the amount of interpersonal contact a person has, and also what purposes and values are involved in such contact.[6] In all the essays of this inquiry the number of groups that the various categories adhere to will be a provoking, if not always a highly revealing, relationship. The questionnaire collected data on both the number of groups that existed in the respondent's community and the number to which he belonged.

The modern and unoccupied occupational groups indicate more groups organized in their localities and also indicate that they have joined more groups. The unoccupied record more groups where they are established, but this might be accounted for by their greater interest

---

[6] For an analysis of Moroccan groups see the author's "Patterns of Group Development in a New Nation: Morocco," *American Political Science Review*, v. 55, no. 2, (June 1961), pp. 321-332. Some comparative material and perhaps the most complete record of related writings on the use of occupational data will be found in the notes and findings of Melvin M. Tumin and Arnold Feldman, *Social Class and Social Change in Puerto Rico*, Princeton, Princeton University Press, 1961, pp. 320-355. The distribution of groups and occupations is significant at the .10 level.

in organization and political activity in general. The more notable contrast is that although more groups are organized in the vicinity of the unoccupied they have tended to join fewer of them. The respondent of modern occupational background appears to have more group contacts, though reporting fewer groups in his locale. The traditionally occupied shows indications of being a selective joiner. At low levels on group participation he is fairly active, but large proportions of the traditional group have no opportunity to join and more than half gave no sign of having any group memberships.

Table II-2
NUMBER OF MEMBERSHIPS AND OCCUPATION BY PERCENTAGES

	Modern *Per Cent (N=31)*	*Traditional* *Per Cent (N=33)*	*Unoccupied* *Per Cent (N=27)*
None°	16	58	33
1 - 2	52	30	44
3 or more	32	12	22
Chi square = .02			

° In this table no responses have been included with no memberships. Many respondents left some of the questions dealing with their membership blank, while filling in others. Since there was no apparent reluctance to note the presence of such groups in these cases, it was assumed that the respondents had no reluctance to record non-membership and presumed that no reply would be taken to mean they did not belong to the groups whose presence they had noted.

The group characteristics of the occupational categories raise questions that can be partially dealt with using the available data. First, it may be that membership is simply a function of the presence of groups in each occupational category. Regardless of occupation, the party secretaries who are near organized groups may join while those that find it inconvenient or simply impossible to join do not. To explore this relationship a three variable analysis of groups, memberships and occupations was made. Although the number of cases is small it appears that the memberships of occupational categories relate to the number of organized groups in a reasonable pattern. At both high and low levels of group organization persons in the modern occupational category are most likely to join groups. At the higher levels of group organization, nearly half those of modern occupational background acquire outside memberships more frequently where more groups exist. The traditionally occupied are less likely to join groups even where more have been organized.

Perspectives of a Moroccan Nationalist

A second argument that might be used to question the findings in Table II - 2 is that the total results conceal the fact that the traditionally occupied may be more active in their region of concentration. Again the groupings are small in a three variable distribution, but the relationship between membership, province and occupation has been explored. The findings indicate that the occupational groupings responded as previously suggested regardless of province. Those in modern pursuits are very likely to have more memberships in both regional settings. The traditional are least likely to join in advanced regions and also in retarded regions. The results for the unoccupied are of doubtful value because of the small number in retarded provinces, but the available cases are distributed as expected.

Educational background, which will be studied in more detail in the next essay, is also extremely helpful in explaining the role of the unoccupied and testifies to what is probably the most important single characteristic of the traditionally occupied. Very few of those in traditional occupation have had more than a Koranic school education, but nearly half of the unoccupied and nearly two-thirds of the modern occupational group have enjoyed some advanced education. University education is heavily concentrated in the modern occupational group, but secondary education is roughly equally divided between the modern and unoccupied groups. The source of the secondary education in these two groups is helpful in explaining their respective occupations. More than half of the modern group with secondary education went to government-sponsored schools, but more than two-thirds (seven of ten cases) of the unoccupied went to the party free schools. This lends more support to the hypothesis that the unoccupied are full-time, party supported cadre. At the very minimum it makes their full-time devotion to party affairs more understandable.

There are important differences in the age structure of the three occupational groups, although the findings might be anticipated from

Table II-3

EDUCATION AND OCCUPATION BY PERCENTAGES

	Modern Per Cent (N=27)	Traditional Per Cent (N=27)	Unoccupied Per Cent (N=23)
Elementary	30	81	53
Secondary	37	11	43
University	33	7	4

Chi square = .0001

what has already been learned of each group. The results are summarized in Table II-4. Each occupational group has readily distinguishable age characteristics, although the differences are less pronounced in the modern occupational group. Those in modern occupations are concentrated on the middle age group. The traditionally occupied group is considerably older than the other groups. The small percentage of young persons suggests the growing attractions of other occupations and the decline in proportionate importance of traditional pursuits as the new country undergoes social change. It also suggests that the party, which did not rely heavily on traditionally occupied persons at an early date as shown above, has recently tended to recruit elder, traditional persons to work under the younger party officials with modern occupa·tional background. The potential organizational conflict is apparent. The fact that the Istiqlal relied more heavily on emotional, religious appeals as time passed suggests that there may have indeed been important discontinuites in communication.

Table II-4

AGE AND OCCUPATION BY PERCENTAGES

	Modern Per Cent (N=30)	Traditional Per Cent (N=33)	Unoccupied Per Cent (N=26)
30 years or under	27	21	46
31-40 years	43	36	42
Over 40 years	30	42	12

Chi square = .10

From these facts the image of the unoccupied as the full-time party worker becomes clearer, and the group may even be those whose contact with politics is entirely party oriented. Much of their adult lives has been spent in party office and they took office much earlier in their lives than other occupational groups. The modern occupational group was most important in the early organization of the Istiqlal and was recruited at the earliest date. However, they tended to take office later and are very likely not as totally committed to the party as the unoccupied seem to be. The Istiqlal also seems to get fewer of modern occupational background as time passes, an important potential source of conflict within the party as well as general party weakness as other parties emerge in Morocco. If those in modern occupations tend to be more absorbed in their work and engage in pursuits that give the secretaries satisfaction and rewards outside the Istiqlal, which seems reasonable, there may well be tendencies toward the formation of a professional cadre. The traditionally oriented are the oldest and the least experienced. Thus, the young and fully committed persons, largely of party background and often educated at party expense, may come to be the dominant persons in the post-independence nationalist party.

PARTY POSITION AND OCCUPATION

The party secretaries' social background reveals the vast differences that a nationalist party must accommodate in its own organization. In addition to these complications, which are considerably more than those encountered in a national party in a more highly developed country, there is a long organizational history to the party. Given the restrictions on social mobility found in most new countries plus the high motivation of most nationalist militants, it seems very likely that severe internal conflicts can occur. Indeed, even party leaders are not immune to such strains, and the Istiqlal forfeited its unity to factional interests in early 1959.

The party clearly preferred persons of modern occupational background in the early phase of organization. Moreover, it is noteworthy that fewer modern occupational types are becoming party secretaries as time passes as indicated in Table II-5. This may be a function of the party's awareness of its past reliance on the modern occupations as well as the many attractions that take persons of more advanced qualifications away from party activity as the country develops. The findings would be less meaningful if the modern occupational group was concentrated in the regions first organized, i.e., the more advanced provinces, and the traditional group in areas that were later organized. This appears to be the case for the traditional occupational group, but the modern group is scattered in advanced and less advanced provinces.

Table II-5

DATE OF ORGANIZATION AND OCCUPATION BY PERCENTAGES

	Modern Per Cent (N=29)	*Traditional* Per Cent (N=43)	*Unoccupied* Per Cent (N=26)
To 1956	45	27	35
1956	34	55	42
1957 on	21	18	23

Chi square not significant.

Although the sample is quite small for three variable breakdowns, a table was made holding provincial groupings constant. In the advanced provinces, both modern and traditional occupational groups appear to have been included in newly organized offices at about the same rate. Thus, one may conclude that no occupational group prevailed as the party grew in the advanced provinces, but that modern occupations were most likely to be represented first in the organization of retarded provinces. The point is an important one in view of the history of the party, which has generally given more attention to the views of elder, more traditional leaders. Serious differences might easily arise between elder leaders and the lower party officials of modern occupational background, who were the Istiqlal's first strong supporters in the early period of independence. The party's failure to cultivate traditionally occupied persons in remote provinces may have also contributed to the party's visible weakness during the tribal riots of late 1958.

The results of the analysis of organizational dates and occupation are generally confirmed by a similar analysis of recruitment dates. Although the time span is longer, Table II-6 demonstrates that it was not until 1955 that the Istiqlal began to recruit persons in traditional occupations in large numbers, while approximately half of both modern and unoccupied occupational groups joined the party before 1948. The year 1948 was chosen as a breaking point because it marks the end of the party's first major organizational effort. With the arrival of an extremely conservative Resident General and the end of *tripartisme* in France a period of reaction began. The nationalists were treated with varying degrees of tolerance until the exile of the King in 1953, which introduced the period of violence. The clandestine reorganization of the Istiqlal began in 1955 following the release of most of its leaders under the Mendes-France government, and was, of course, continued with vigor from the time the King returned late that year. There were, of course, many factors that favored making contact with and recruiting persons in modern occupations during the Protectorate. However, those in traditional occupations were also in good positions to influence the populace as the movement developed and also had some organizational advantages over other occupational groups. Although the party leader militants found those in modern positions more suitable to the early stages of nationalist organization, the traditionally occupied became more useful and more knowledgeable as time passed. A large share of those

23

recruited at an early date have become the unoccupied party secretaries, thereby indicating that they do indeed represent more experienced and very likely more militant local officials.[7]

Table II-6
DATE OF RECRUITMENT AND OCCUPATION BY PERCENTAGES

	Modern Per Cent (N=31)	Traditional Per Cent (N=31)	Unoccupied Per Cent (N=27)
To 1948	48	26	55
1948-1954	32	32	33
1955 on	19	42	11

Chi square = .05

In evaluating the attitudes of the secretaries their length of time in office may well be the most important consideration. As a party secretary a person takes on prestige and responsibility that very likely orients him more strongly toward the official party line. Thus, it would be helpful to know not only when the office in question was organized and how long the respondent has been in the party, but also how long he has undergone the discipline and indoctrination of party office. For present purposes a single time differentiation has been made at mid-1956.[8] At that time the Istiqlal began a complete overhaul of its ranks and cadre. The present organizational structure was instituted throughout the country, and schools for party militants were set up. Date of office is particularly helpful in locating distinguishing characteristics of the unoccupied party secretaries. Over half of them took office before mid-1956 as compared to about a third of the other occupational groups. The unoccupied secretary may very likely be regarded as a more experienced, and more thoroughly indoctrinated, party official than those in tradi-

---

[7] Again the groupings are too small to make definitive judgments, but a table has been made holding both occupation and province constant. It is possible that early recruitment may rest more with proximity and ease of contact, which would involve the nearer, more advanced provinces, than with occupation. This does not seem to have been the case. Of the eleven persons in retarded provinces having modern occupations, nine were recruited before 1955. Of the thirteen persons in retarded provinces having traditional occupations, eleven were recruited after 1955. In the advanced provinces, however, both occupational groups seem to have been recruited at about the same rate except in the earliest period, which favored modern occupations. Thus, in the more advanced regions those having modern occupations had slightly greater chances of being recruited, while in the less advanced provinces modern occupation made a considerable difference.

[8] Of those in modern occupations, 10 of 26 took office at the earliest date; of the traditional, 10 of 30; and of the unoccupied, 14 of 25. Chi square = .10.

tional and modern occupations. The findings lend strong support to the speculation that the party has indeed developed its own occupational class that is supported through party channels.

Of the occupational groupings the modern group has the largest proportion of secretaries that have held previous office, nearly three-fourths, although they are closely followed by the unoccupied group. As might be expected from the analysis of date of office, the traditionally occupied indicated much less previous attainment of office. Less than half indicated that they had some party office before their present one.[9] Party office is, however, related to the overall level of party organization in the various regions of the country. It might be argued that the poor record of the traditionally occupied is largely a result of their isolation in the countryside and the party's failure to expand in their vicinities. There are two ways that this can be explored within the limits of available data.

The first is to explore the relation of previous office to date of present office. A person who had previous office and also took his present office at an early date is more experienced than one indicating previous office, but not taking office until later. By correlating previous office, date of office and occupation we are able to hold time constant, although not with the accuracy that might be desired for a more decisive analysis. Even allowing for the small groupings of a three variable analysis it appears that the traditional occupational group has a poorer record in both time periods. The modern occupational group had the highest proportion of previous office attainment before mid-1956. After independence and the party reorganization in mid-1956 the unoccupied have the highest proportion of persons with previous office. Thus, holding date of office constant does not greatly affect the previous findings.

A second argument might be that proximity, which would be related to the expansion of the party, was a crucial determinant of the previous office record, and so the traditionally occupied were handicapped. Although the Istiqlal was undoubtedly extremely popular throughout the country by independence, it had been forcefully excluded from many regions by the colonial regime and had been unable to organize ef-

---

[9] The figures for previous office for modern, unoccupied and traditional categories, respectively, are 71 per cent (19 of 27 respondents), 68 per cent (17 of 25), and 47 per cent (14 of 30). Chi square = .05.

fectively under semi-clandestine conditions. To check the relationship of regional characteristics and office and occupation a three variable analysis has been done holding provinces constant. The analysis shows very clearly that proximity was indeed an important factor in gaining experience in party office. The disadvantage that the traditionally occupied have in the party, which has been suggested in several ways in this chapter, appears to depend heavily on their isolation. In the advanced provinces those in traditional occupations have a record of previous party office that is comparable to that of the modern and unoccupied occupational groups. It was in the retarded regions, however, that the traditionally occupied were at a disadvantage as compared with those in modern pursuits. This suggests the hypothesis that occupational differentiation has greater significance, at least in more intense political activity like party organization, only in the retarded regions. Contrary to the widely accepted belief, it is modern occupational background that appears to have been most important in more remote, retarded provinces. It appears that party office required a degree of sophistication and a measure of managerial skill that the traditionally occupied lacked, even though their occupation and its related characteristics would seem to make them a more effective group in remote areas.

The handicap of the traditionally occupied is clearly evident in their estimates of preparation for higher office. Only forty per cent felt prepared for their present office, while nearly eighty per cent of the more capable modern and more committed unoccupied groups have confidence in their preparation.[10] That the latter group, which has less education than the modern group, should have an equally high estimate of its qualification for office is of special interest and will be explored in more detail later. There are certainly some reasons why this might be the case, even by impersonal criteria, since the unoccupied are very likely more active and more devoted to the Istiqlal. However, it may also account for deterioration in party administration and create internal tensions.

The lack of confidence among the traditionally occupied is also expressed in their aspirations for higher office. Only half of them indicat-

---

[10] The figures for those feeling satisfactorily prepared for present office by modern, traditional, and unoccupied groups, respectively, is 22 of 28 respondents, 12 of 30, and 19 of 24. Not statistically significant.

ed that they would like higher office. In the cases of the modern and unoccupied groups approximately two-thirds aspired to higher office.[11] Although the opportunity was overlooked in the questionnaire, it would be interesting to know in future inquiry if those who are less committed feel that they have alternative aspirations of similar or greater importance. Much of what has been learned about the full-time party secretaries suggests that they are intensely focused on the party and more dependent on it for personal recognition.

The traditionally occupied party official would be more likely to depend on traditional ties of family and religion for personal rewards. This was indicated in the religious self-estimates, which nearly all the officials provided. The most fervent are the traditionally occupied, while the modern occupational group divides almost evenly between fervent and moderate self-evaluations. The most important finding is admission by the unoccupied group that they are nearly all less than fervent.[12] This is important in evaluating the extent to which they do represent a body of effective party organizers, especially in the remote regions where the party depended on them most heavily and where conflict with tradition could be more acute. The religious self-evaluations make it clear that where religion enters into Moroccan political life, sharp differences could arise between certain groups of party officials.

The last background characteristic to be briefly analyzed in relation to occupation is participation in the clandestine, resistance organization. Although ostensibly under Istiqlal auspices, an almost completely new organization was built after the exile of the King and the arrest of most known party officials in late 1953. Many of these persons objected to the terms on which Morocco achieved her independence and held the Istiqlal responsible. There are probably very few such persons represented here, which means that one would be likely to get opinions from resistance participants who accepted the government. Nevertheless, the available data are extremely valuable. Persons who were active in the resistance are very difficult to make contact with under any circumstan-

---

11 The findings for aspiration to higher office for traditional, modern, and unoccupied groups, respectively, is 14 of 27 respondents, 19 of 29, and 17 of 27. Chi square is not significant.

12 Findings for fervent evaluations for the modern, traditional, and unoccupied groups, respectively, are 48 per cent (15 of 31 respondents), 66 per cent (21 of 31), and 16 per cent (4 of 25). Chi square = .001.

ces, even since independence, and when drawn out are reluctant to express how their experience in organized violence may relate to their present views. Since it appears that there will be more participants in new political systems who have terrorist backgrounds some care has been given to learning as much as possible about those found in the Istiqlal.

Approximately the same proportion of those in modern and unoccupied occupational categories participated in the resistance or its rural auxiliary force, the Moroccan Army of Liberation. At least half of the party officials in the modern and unoccupied categories were involved in the violent resistance to the French regime.[13] The importance of modern occupational background might be expected, of course, since considerable skill and initiative were needed to evade the police and army networks organized by the French. A certain amount of sheer technical knowledge was also needed to work with the weapons and communications of the clandestine organization. For these reasons the traditionally occupied may have necessarily been less active. Slightly more than a fourth of those in traditional pursuits were in one or both terrorist organizations. The findings, however, do not allow for the concentration of the resistance in the advanced provinces where, first, the French and French installations were concentrated, and second, the resistance could find sufficient friends and supporters to operate over long periods of time. The occupational distinction would be salient only if it can be shown that the traditionally occupied did not participate even where opportunity and motivation existed.

To test this relationship a three variable breakdown was made holding provincial characteristics constant. The modern occupational group still appears to have performed better in both the retarded and advanced provinces. However, in the advanced setting the traditional and the unoccupied groups have about the same record, which suggests that both groups had certain handicaps in the resistance. The great disadvantage of being remote from the resistance organizations is also strikingly evident in the isolation of the traditionally occupied in the retarded provinces, none of whom joined in the resistance. Being in a

---

[13] The findings on resistance participation for the modern, unoccupied and traditional groups, respectively, are 60 per cent (17 of 29 respondents), 50 per cent (12 of 24), and 27 per cent (8 of 30). Chi square = .01.

distant province was definitely a handicap, but having a modern occupation was also clearly advantageous even in the advanced provinces.

The analysis of occupational differences among the local officials broaches several important problems of the nationalist party in transition, and also highlights some other problems of continuing interest in this study.[14] With very little embellishment the data reveal the many potential sources of tension confronting a nationalist party in a rapidly developing country. Those with modern occupations, skills, and knowledge have clearly held key roles in the past, but there are several indications that fewer persons with modern skills are now interested in nationalist politics. There are very likely more secure and more remunerative opportunities in other sectors of Moroccan life. Those with traditional experience of various kinds are coming into their own, especially in the more remote provinces. However, there are undoubtedly a multitude of problems to be solved before they can function smoothly in a national organization of any kind. There are, of course, many ways in which the more recently recruited, less confident traditionally occupied secretary may feel anxiety in his office. As for the full-time secretaries, the available data suggest that a professional cadre grew within the Istiqlal, and with it many problems of bureaucratic control and supervision.

Looking at those with modern occupations, their historic importance in the Istiqlal can be seen in their tendency to be recruited before independence and to take office before or immediately after independence. There are many things that may take their attention away from party affairs in addition to their specialized occupational capacities. They tend to join more groups outside the party and they, in turn, probably find many outlets for their ambitions and interests in addition to the Istiqlal. Although their ages are fairly evenly distributed, more recently fewer young persons in modern occupations appear to be recruited compared with other occupational groups. They are more experienced in office and are aware of the value of their experience. The demographic variations within the modern occupational group are to some extent assurance of their moderation and variety of interest. In general, they

---

[14] The student wishing to compare occupational differences in Morocco with some of the findings about occupation and political behavior in the United States and other advanced nations will find a summary in Robert E. Lane, *Political Life: How People Get Involved in Politics*, Glencoe, Free Press, 1959, pp. 331-334, or Seymour Martin Lipset, *Political Man*, New York, Doubleday, 1960, pp. 179-219.

appear to be those most likely to express their interests clearly and to weigh evidence in more realistic terms.

The local officials in traditional occupations have suffered a major handicap as a result of their geographical isolation. In itself this is not a startling conclusion, but the analysis permits further investigation. In several instances, e.g., resistance participation, it appears that the traditionally occupied were able to overcome any disadvantage their occupational position entailed. However, the hurdles of the transition to a more advanced social setting are many. Even where the traditionally occupied have had equal opportunity to join more groups outside the party they have tended to lag behind the other two groups. Although they usually joined the party later and were not in office on a large scale until late 1956, they are older. Thus, the party seems to have incorporated many local officials with less preparation, who are also at a stage of life where the acquisition of new skills is difficult. The traditionally occupied are clearly aware of their poor preparation for office, and in many cases do not aspire to higher office. They are, on the whole, a group whose value to the party is mixed at the very best. They may be able to appeal to the populace more easily in areas of the country where the party is weak, but they have less confidenec and less ability than most other officials. It is entirely possible that they do not understand the needs of a modern nation, and that their values conflict with the secular trends associated with modernization.

The unoccupied secretaries are perhaps the most valuable discovery of the inquiry, for they are not easily visible or even identifiable in field work in the country. They also denote a trend toward bureaucratization of the party, which played in the split of the Istiqlal in early 1959. Their dependence on the party, at least psychologically, is apparent in their early recruitment despite their generally young ages. Often they appear to be party youth, who have been politicized entirely within the party and who took office quite early in the transition to independence. As experienced and ambitious officials they have probably acquired a sophistication beyond their educational level. They are eager joiners of outside groups despite their focus on party affairs. Considering the importance of religious leaders in the Istiqlal, it is curious to note that many of the party's most active officials regard themselves as moderately religious Muslims.

III

Divergence and Discontinuity in Education

Of the nationalist goals none are sought with more determination than increased educational opportunity. In a way that is curiously parallel to the nineteenth century reformers, the nationalists have thought of education as the solution to most of their social and economic problems, and have often assumed that the absence of educational facilities created their problems. There is a fair measure of undeniable truth in both these allegations, but education alone is hardly an explanation for all the ills and crises of the developing nations. After independence, education has remained one of the prominent goals of nationalist governments. One of the most ambitious, if not entirely successful, programs of the new Moroccan government has been the expansion of educational opportunity. Since independence, Morocco has allocated approximately a sixth of her national expenditure to education, which has ranked only after defense and the economy in its share of the total budget.

The effort that has been made is testimony to the sincerity with which Moroccans view education. For the nationalists the high esteem attached to education is doubly entrenched, for the Istiqlal has its original impulse from what was in one sense a pedagogical problem. The famous, or possibly infamous in Moroccan eyes, "Berber *dahir*" (law) of 1930 marks the beginning of popularized nationalism, although small intellectual groups had existed before the time. The young students of Paris under Ahmed Balafrej and the ulema (religious scholars) of Qarawiyn University under Allal Al-Fassi considered the new law a threat to their entire culture. The law would have emphasized and preserved differences between the coastal and tribal areas, and was to be reinforced by educational reforms that would discourage the use of Arabic in the countryside and create a rural elite. The country's educational needs were underscored as the struggle for independence progressed. The nationalist leaders often found themselves without educated lieutenants, who were needed for organizational purposes and also as evidence of the country's readiness for self-rule.

The educational deficiencies that hampered the nationalists before independence continue to do so, and have left a deep impression. The Istiqlal would never have succeeded without the cadre of partially trained persons who served as local secretaries. To counteract the effects of French education, the party sponsored "free schools" to provide instruction in Arabic and to increase the numbers of young people qualified for higher education. The schools also served as recruiting and indoctrination centers before independence. Over a tenth (43) of all those answering the questionnaire indicated attendance at party-run schools. Nearly a fourth (93) of the questionnaire's total return came from persons with over eleven years in the traditional, Koranic school and roughly a third of all those in modern occupations were school teachers in modernized schools. The entire development of modern Morocco is indelibly associated with the educational advancement so that it is well worthwhile seeing how the educated have contributed and how educational differences have played in nationalist politics.

As outlined in Table I - 2, the analysis sample includes a higher proportion of persons with advanced education than the discarded group of responses. In reference to the total return of the questionnaire, about two-thirds of those with university education, about one-half of those with secondary education, and about one-fourth of those with a traditional, elementary education are included in the smaller sample. Although fourteen persons of the small sample did not give their educational experience (their reluctance to do so while replying to other more intimate queries suggests the importance attached to education), it was thought a sufficiently important variable to proceed with the reduced sample of seventy-nine persons. A further complication in the processing should be noted. A large group of persons (43) had a Koranic school education and a fairly large group (24) had been to a secondary school of the party or the government, but only twelve persons had university education. The small number means that a single division may produce a very small sub-group and that a three variable analysis must often be interpreted as reliable for only the larger sub-group.

SOCIAL BACKGROUND AND EDUCATION

The provincial distribution by educational groups reveals tendencies that might be expected. The least educated are more concentrated in the retarded provinces, while increasing degrees of education bring increasing concentration in more advanced provinces. The rural-urban distinction also shows that although many of those with elementary education are located in advanced provinces they tend to be heavily concentrated in the rural villages.[1] Those with secondary education are also heavily concentrated in the villages, and only those with university education appear to have a fifty-fifty chance of settling in a city. The findings reinforce earlier speculation on the value of the sample as an indicator of rural opinion. It should be understood, however, that the distribution of educational groupings in the rural areas for the country as a whole is not nearly as favorable as appears in the analysis of the party secretaries. Indeed, the findings suggest that the Istiqlal may have been instrumental in allocating more better-educated persons to remote areas than might have otherwise occurred.

Table III-1
PROVINCIAL DISTRIBUTION AND EDUCATION BY PERCENTAGES

	Elementary Per Cent (N=43)	*Secondary* Per cent (N=24)	*University* Per Cent (N=12)
Advanced	65	79	75
Retarded	35	21	25

Chi square not significant.

Educational achievement has long been associated with the individual's rate of interaction with others. Although the sub-groups are very small, the findings indicate that the more highly educated persons are generally located in places where more nationally organized groups exist.[2] The higher level of group development associated with higher education suggests the possibility that such persons are a requisite to

---

[1] For the elementary, secondary, and university educated groups, respectively 87 per cent (38 of 43), 71 per cent (17 of 24), and 59 per cent (7 of 12) were in villages. Chi square is not significant.

[2] In the elementary, secondary, and university categories 30 per cent (13 of 43

group development. Although the less privileged educational group may not stimulate group formation, the less educated may be quite willing to join where groups have been formed. In a three variable analysis by province it apeared that in the advanced provinces group activities were available to all educational groups. Having established that there were comparable openings for membership, the next question was whether the educational groups actually became members. Before doing so the relation between membership and education should also be noted.

The distribution of educational achievement and memberships, given in Table III - 2, strongly suggests that education may be an important requisite in creating the willingness and interest represented by joining a group. If this is proved to be the case more widely than the present sample permits, much of the theorizing about the formation of groups as an aid to increased political participation in underdeveloped countries should be reconsidered. However, in advanced areas where groups are more accessible to all and where there is very likely more encouragement to join, the less educated appear capable of acquiring memberships with some ease. In the advanced provinces about two-thirds in the elementary educational category had some group memberships. In the same provinces nearly all secretaries with some advanced education indicated some memberships outside the party. It is quite possible, of course, that there is also a pattern of selective adherence, which is not revealed by the data. The less educated may, for example, be much more active in the illiteracy groups. However, the less educated person does not join groups at a high rate even when the opportunity exists, although he does seem to acquire one or two memberships quite easily. The person with a secondary education appears to have about a fifty-fifty chance of greatly increasing this membership as more groups are organized.

Table III-2

NUMBER OF MEMBERSHIPS AND EDUCATION BY PERCENTAGES

	Elementary Per Cent (N=43)	Secondary Per cent (N=24)	University Per Cent (N=12)
0-2	91	58	67
3 or more	9	42	33

Chi square = .0001

---

respondents), 58 per cent (14 of 24), and 58 per cent (7 of 12), respectively, indicated the presence of five or more nationally organized groups. Chi square = .05.

Since the number of memberships of the developing citizen may be an important indicator in estimating political trends in a new country, several other dstributions were made to see how the education and membership categories related to other factors. It might be argued, first, that age compensates for education and, therefore, the elder persons would tend to join more groups regardless of education. Such an argument has obvious limitations in a rapidly changing society, although the study encompasses three years of development and the respondents are persons of more than average interest in their fellow citizens and country. Neither youth nor maturity seem to be compensating factors, although there are fragmentary indications that younger persons of secondary education and middle-aged persons of elementary education are more likely to join groups.

A second possible argument is that reading might make up for education where the party secretary of less educational achievement has the interest and time to seek his own information. This, in turn, might be reasonably expected to increase the secretary's likelihood to join organized groups or to take part in starting groups. Again the results do not yield large enough groupings to be highly reliable, but they are extremely suggestive. The high correlation between membership in groups and reading among the more highly educated might be anticipated, but nevertheless contrasts sharply with the distribution found for elementary education. Even those with less schooling who read more do not appear to join or to help form more groups. It should also be noted, however, that quite a large proportion of those with elementary education who read very little also join groups. It is possible that the social relationship reverses under different circumstances, i.e., the secretaries appear to be gaining sophistication and come to appreciate a group with or without the stimulus of more reading. In any event increased reading correlates with increased memberships only among those respondents having some advanced education.

The relation between occupation and education has already been discussed and the findings given in Table II - 3. In a retarded society one would expect that education would contribute to acquiring better occupations, as it clearly has in this study. There is, however, a reverse relationship that should be noted, which is particularly evident in the case of the Istiqlal inquiry. The educational needs of the rapidly developing country are so great that avenues of occupational advancement may be devised quite independent of educational qualificàtion. This is especially important in the local politics of a new nation, since few well-educated persons are content with the relatively obscure and under-paid positions offered to party secretaries and other local political of-fices. For many persons politics has very likely become a vocation and their educational qualifications, if any, are being used in only an in-direct manner. Much more research is needed to comprehend fully the social mobility effects of nationalist politics, but social advancement from the lower levels of the party does not appear as easy as the brilliant success of a few national leaders might suggest.

Language skill has always been associated with education and the relationship appears to hold true in the developing country. Those with elementary and secondary education averaged slightly less than one language apiece in addition to their knowledge of Maghrebi Arabic, but the university products average almost two languages in addition to their native tongue and three of them knew three languages. There was, how-ever, an important difference in the composition of the language com-petence given by elementary and secondary educational groups. Nearly half of the former indicated some knowledge of a Berber dialect and about a third had some knowledge of classical Arabic. Those with sec-ondary education had more classical Arabic, which two-thirds of them noted, and almost no Berber skill. None of the university people indicat-ed Berber as their sole language although about half were bilingual. Any interpretation placed on these findings should take into account the Ara-bization process which Morocco has been undergoing since the ninth century. Berber never developed a written form and will be of less importance in the future.

Modern education in Morocco dates, at the earliest, from the Protec-torate and did not achieve a scale capable of transforming the country until after World War II. Even in the last two decades, however, higher education was centered in France and secondary education was consid-ered inadequate by the nationalists. To some extent drawing a sample from any developing country means that there are few young persons with a university education and few elder persons with secondary edu-cation. With this development characteristic in mind, the comparison of age and education among local officials may help identify party tensions. For the segment of Moroccans considered here, secondary education is probably the crucial point of advancement.

The findings are most suggestive of political trends in the country as a whole and also of the problems of the party. The Istiqlal's local cadre has been made up largely of middle-aged (30-40 years) persons with a traditional education. Nearly a fourth of all the local secretaries sampled fall into this category and, if the elder secretaries of the same education are included, nearly half the secretaries have traditional background and elementary education. Actually the proportions are probably much greater since those respondents who have been discarded would undoubtedly be concentrated in the elementary group, as shown in Table I - 2. It should also be noted that judging from age levels the party seems to be recruiting fewer young persons of elementary educational background for local office, or possibly finds that age compensates for lack of education. In the more remote provinces, where the less educated are found, age also commands respect. In the secondary educational group the age composition is nearly reversed. Well over half of them are thirty years of age or less and the proportions decrease with the older age groups, as the educational experience of the country would lead one to expect.

Two additional distributions were made to explore what other relation age and education might have to party position. When considered in reference to previously holding office, it was found that there was a tendency for older persons with elementary education to have had less experience. Their experience, however, was not too different from those having secondary education, where half of the youngest age group had not had previous office. The second distribution was made in reference to aspiration for higher office. In the case of elementary education approximately two-thirds of both the middle-age group and the elder age group aspired to higher office. For the youngest sub-group having secondary education, there were signs of considerably higher aspirations. More than eighty per cent aspired to higher office. (Although the number of respondents in the older age cells is negligible, it is interesting that they were the only cells where less than half of the respondents aspired to higher office.) This provides some grounds for arguing that age and education relate inversely to aspiration for office, a pattern of behavior that may very likely create awkward internal problems for the Istiqlal, and that may have contributed to the tensions splitting the party in 1959.

PARTY POSITION AND EDUCATION

Although education may be the key to social advancement in the developing country, it does not necessarily mean that more responsible, more civic-minded citizens are being created. Even the relatively well defined set of values governing the Istiqlal did not serve to preclude destructive internal tension. The party, like most other national political activities, meant many different things to party militants in different social positions. Naturally education has had an important effect on the respondents' evaluation of their training for present and higher office. The comparison of education and preparation for office underscores some problems of how those in the intermediate educational positions relate themselves to the party and, more generally, to national politics.

Those having only elementary education were the least confident of their ability in their present office and in higher office, but all the educational groups indicated higher judgment of their qualification than

Table III-3
AGE AND EDUCATION BY PERCENTAGES

	Elementary Per Cent (N=43)	Secondary Per cent (N=24)	University Per Cent (N=12)
30 years or under	9	66	25
30-40 years	56	21	42
over 40 years	35	12	33
Chi square = .001			

might be expected in a country where the party system is not yet highly specialized. It is quite possible that having joined the party and made the initial commitment of taking office constitutes the crucial step in the individual's judgment of himself and the establishment of his self-confidence. This is a question that merits further investigation because of its importance to our general knowledge of the politics of the developing countries.[3]

---

[3] In some respects, the psychological impact of increased education may be very similar regardless of cultural differences. The comparative implications of these findings are suggested in the more detailed findings of Angus Campbell, Philip E. Converse, Warren E. Miller, and Donald E. Stokes, *The American Voter*, New York, Wiley, 1960, pp. 475-481.

The least educated group is also notable for the large proportion that consider themselves totally unprepared. Slightly more than a third of the least educated judged themselves unqualified for their present *and* higher office. The self-evaluations of those with secondary education were made very diffrently. Of the twenty-four persons only one person felt totally disqualified for both offices, and nearly two-thirds felt fully qualified in terms of both present and higher office. Thus, the data show that the traditionally educated are quite aware of their less adequate preparation for office. In the university group there is an understandably high percentage who feel fully qualified and a very small percentage who feel disqualified in either of the two contexts raised by the question. Although the size of the university group makes more general conclusions risky, it is interesting that proportionately fewer with university education than with secondary education feel well qualified.

Despite the differences in the evaluations of preparation for office, the educational groups feel rather alike when judging their aspiration for office. The findings raise some intriguing questions since a larger proportion of the least educated aspire for higher office than feel qualified for present or higher office. Conversely, for the two more highly-educated groups there are fewer persons indicating a desire for higher office than prepared according to their own judgment of their preparation. These questions will be further investigated in a later chapter. One observation concerning educational differentiation can be made. Local party officials differ greatly in evaluating their educational qualifications in relation to their future in the party. It appears that the less educated give education little weight and the more educated give it more weight.

The Istiqlal has also had a large number of internal organizational problems in getting the best qualified local official in the right position. Because the lower party offices are predominantly part-time posts, the party has depended heavily on the human resources of the local community, and could not easily encourage more talented, or politically ambitious secretaries to move in order to put themselves in better positions for party advancement. Although the party has a reasonable, if not adequate, number of more highly educated party secretaries, it does not appear that the party has succeeded in putting them into positions of greater responsibility. A local official appears to have had about a fifty-fifty chance of achieving the higher post of section secretary regardless of education.

The secretaries with elementary education have a fifty-fifty chance (eighteen of thirty-six cases) of becoming a section official in the rural setting, but the chances are not considerably greater for a person with secondary education (eleven of seventeen cases) and only slightly greater for the university educated (seven of twelve cases). It appears that the Istiqlal is in such need of leaders in the rural areas that lack of education is little handicap in seeking office. There is also a greater likelihood, of course, that more highly educated persons will have additional interests which attract them more than party responsibility. However, the findings provide reason to inquire further as to whether the Istiqlal has itself yet achieved sufficient organizational skill to place or to attract more highly qualified persons in positions of greater responsibility.

Table III-4
DATE OF ATTAINING OFFICE AND EDUCATION BY PERCENTAGES

	Elementary *Per Cent (N=43)*	*Secondary* *Per Cent (N=21)*	*University* *Per Cent (N=10)*
To 1956	21	24	20
1956	39	52	50
1957 or after	39	24	30

Chi square not significant.

The tendency to rely heavily on less educated party secretaries is also clearly in evidence in the analysis of date of office.[4] The two more highly educated groups were drawn most heavily into party office during the party overhaul of 1956 and appear to be of less significance since that time. The least educated seem to have become increasingly important, although more evidence would be needed for a conclusive finding. Their relative increase might be explained away by the Istiqlal's expansion into more retarded areas, where it had to be content with less qualified secretaries. This possibility was checked by comparing date of attaining office, education and provincial setting, although the subgroupings are small. In 1956 eight secretaries with elementary educational background were appointed in retarded areas, while fourteen took of-

---

[4] To meet the need for trained party officials, special schools were held in the summer of 1956 and 1957. The same thing was done by the trade unions and other groups that hoped to have national organizations. The problem is discussed in more detail in the author's *Political Change in Morocco*, Princeton, Princeton University Press, 1961, pp. 236-240.

fice in more advanced provinces. Thus, the less educated appear to form a larger total percentage of those more recently taking office in advanced as well as retarded provinces.[5]

The trend toward increasing reliance on less educated officials is most noticeable in reference to date of recruitment. The party has, of course, gone through immeasurable changes from the small, select group of intellectuals on which it was based before World War II. The small sample includes only ten persons of pre-war vintage, of whom nine are included in the education groupings. Past reliance on intellectuals is suggested by four of these nine persons having a university education. In each of the three recruitment periods the Istiqlal drew about the same extent on those with less education, but it should be noted that the periods are not equivalent and that recent recruitment is heavily focused on less educated persons. The first period runs from the founding of the party to the post-war reorganization, the second includes six years (1948-1954) and the last slightly more than three years (1955-1958). In the early years the party recruited many more persons with secondary edu-

Table III-5

DATE OF RECRUITMENT AND EDUCATION BY PERCENTAGES

	Elementary Per Cent (N=43)	Secondary Per Cent (N=21)	University Per Cent (N=12)
To 1948	35	42	66
1948-1954	32	29	25
1955 on	32	29	9

Chi square not significant.

cation. The largest differences, though probably inconclusive because of the small sample, have been in the recruitment of university educated people. Of the university group two-thirds were recruited before 1948 and nearly nine-tenths before independence. The findings may be exaggerated to some extent by the additional attractions luring educated persons away from party work over the past two decades, but they are nevertheless dramatic evidence of how difficult it is to get highly skilled

---

[5] The organizational overhaul of the Istiqlal was largely under the impulse of the energetic young leader, Mehdi Ben Barka, who has since left the party and is one of the driving forces in the U.N.F.P. *(Union Nationale des Forces Populaires)*. Ben Barka also began a revision of the cell system of the party, which was designed to maximize the organizational effect of party militants and to isolate them for more intensive indoctrination and training. The failure to adopt these and other reforms contributed to the Istiqlal's split in early 1959.

persons to work in lower positions in the party.[6] This trend has far-reaching implications for the general political development of the country and also increases the influence of the few highly educated persons who are willing to devote time and effort to the party. In practice, this has meant that those with modern advanced education tend to join the upper ranks of the government, while the party's upper hierarchy tends to be dominated with graduates of Muslim universities.

The problems of acquiring and placing party personnel might be alleviated somewhat by skilled management. There is little doubt but that much of the Istiqlal's success has been the result of superior direction and ample resources, but this does not mean that the effort has been made as skillfully as possible. Careful allocation of the inspectors' efforts could compensate for educational shortcomings at lower levels. The overall findings on the frequency of inspector visits indicate that the inspectors distributed their personal attention quite evenly.[7] The least educated received a high proportion of frequent visits, while the university educated are most frequently visited and those with secondary education least frequently visited. A trivariate analysis showed that the inspectors had high frequency exchange with the least educated secretaries in both advanced and retarded provinces. The results of the section and sub-section breakdown were similar. Once again the inspectors appear to have had high rates of contact with the less educated regardless of their hierarchical position.

The findings dispel the possibility that the party inspectors have tended to give more attention to those secretaries having similar educational background, and, on the contrary, point out that the inspectors have probably made an effort to focus their efforts among those local officials having less training. The results also suggest that the secretaries having a traditional education have quite possibly been more influenced by the inspectors, and hence, presumably by the party-line, in

---

[6] In off moments, young educated Moroccans will admit that very few of their group are prepared to work any place but the capital, Rabat, or Casablanca. At one time the college students' organization noted in its motions that they had failed to participate in summer rural development programs and did not display sufficient self-sacrifice.

[7] In the elementary, secondary, and university 45 per cent (18 of 40 respondents), 37 per cent (9 of 34), and 58 per cent (7 of 12), respectively, indicated they had received 3 or more visits over the past six months. Chi square not significant.

forming their opinions than the more educated secretaries. The latter are also likely to be more critical, to exercise their own judgment more forcefully and to have other sources of information.

In some respects the analysis of educational differentiation in the lower ranks of the Istiqlal brings the potential sources of conflict and tension closer than the analysis of occupational differences. Occupation helps relate the party cadre to general knowledge of the social structure of the country, but from the viewpoint of internal party affairs education may more meaningfully reflect the problems facing the nationalist party in a newly independent nation. In a country where survival can still become a major concern it is a considerable accomplishment to be reasonably certain you will be cared for in emergencies, and perhaps receive other favors and opportunities by holding office in the major nationalist party. Education probably has more significance in determining a wide range of political values and expectations. It may even be a means of gaining occupational mobility, as suggested by Table II-3. In the underdeveloped country that has begun to modernize, education is generally respected highly, and those who have acquired some advanced education are reasonably certain of employment and recognition.[8]

For these reasons educational differences may be an especially reliable means of anticipating and isolating sources of tension within the party. This is particularly so in the case of the Istiqlal, where small numbers of persons with advanced education are working with many others who have only a traditional, *musiid* education. The analysis established several points of potential conflict. The bulk of the cadre in the retarded provinces have only elementary education, and it is in these provinces that the Istiqlal is weakest. Furthermore, the rural officials with elementary education tend to be older, while their colleagues and many of their supervisors are young. A surprisingly large percentage of the less educated officials feel that they are sufficiently trained for their present office, though not as many as in the case of better educated

---

[8] Probably the most exhaustive study of the role of education in a developing nation is the study of Melvin M. Tumin and Arnold Feldman, *Social Class and Social Change in Puerto Rico*, Princeton, Princeton University Press 1961. There has been relatively little precise study of the impact of education on the Middle Easterner's attitudes. For a suggestive analysis see George L. Fetter's *Attitudes Toward Selected Aspects of Rural Life and Technical Change Among Central Beka's Farmers'* Beirut, American University Technical Publication No. 13, 1961.

secretaries. Even so the fact that many feel prepared plus the fact that about half the less educated also aspire to higher office points up the kind of problem the Istiqlal may have had.

The irresistible pressures to put those with elementary education in local office are certainly understandable. There were simply not enough well-qualified persons to fill the positions of a greatly expanded nationalist party after independence. The difficulties this may create for the internal administration of the Istiqlal are not fully known, nor is the party likely to engage in the kind of public self-criticism that would increase our knowledge. However, it is interesting to note that a local official seems to have had roughly a fifty-fifty chance of being promoted to the level of section secretary regardless of education. The party has probably had little choice in this, but it does reflect the inadequacies of the Istiqlal's internal administration and the obstacles encountered by a national organization trying to work within a village-rooted society. Many better educated persons are not being fully utilized, perhaps by choice, while the less educated persons may, in fact, be doing little to prepare the party's following for the stresses of modernization and the increasing party competition in Morocco. In some cases they may have even been more of a hazard than a help.

In addition to providing some insight into the kind of conflicts and administrative problems the Istiqlal has faced, the data give us some idea of how the educational groups look upon the party and Moroccan politics. Those with elementary education most recently took office, and there are indications that the party relied on them increasingly as time passed. Some of these persons were recruited early in the party's history, most of them in the advanced provinces. More recently they have been recruited very heavily in retarded provinces. This experience contrasts with the careers of the secretaries who have secondary education. Most of them were very early Istiqlal recruits, and they frequently took office during the crucial reorganization of mid-1956. It seems fairly clear that the Istiqlal has depended on these persons, and, indeed, has educated many of them with party funds.

The findings on social participation are consistent with those uncovered through the analysis of occupational differentiation. The generally less advanced secretary does not acquire membership outside the party to nearly the extent that his more highly educated colleagues do so. Those with secondary education behave quite differently. Where there are opportunities to join more groups the secretary with some secondary education frequently participates in other groups enthusiastically. There is some fragmentary evidence suggesting that such secretaries may even join more associations than the university educated local official. The general conclusion is supported by the analysis of occupational differences, and indicates that more widespread participation in the social and political affairs of a new country may be much more difficult to accomplish than has been anticipated. There may well be a critical level of advancement and individual sophistication which must be reached before a person has the confidence, interest and desire to participate in specialized, voluntary associations. This speculation has additional support from the fact that the sample is persons who, relative to their less privileged compatriots, have had important advantages. Despite the encouragement and support given by the Istiqlal, group activity has not prospered.

IV

Submersion of Linguistic Distinctions

The Berber-Arab distinction has been mentioned several times in discussing linguistic differences. Except for a few remote mountain strongholds the language difference is nearly all that remains to distinguish the two races that have struggled over North Africa for nearly a millennium.[1] Today Moroccans intermarry freely as they have for centuries and there is no racial feeling that approaches the intense hatred found in the presumably more advanced nations. Nevertheless, differences between Berber and Arab have played in contemporary Moroccan politics and also in Protectorate politics, to the discredit of the colonial tutors who sometimes defended intervention by their intention to bring the blessings of a materially more advanced civilization to the Maghreb.

The general pattern of the colonial tactic was contained in the Berber *dahir* of 1930, which hoped to preserve tribal customs in the more retarded regions. While some of the persons who supported the proposal may not have foreseen its ultimate political effect, it served to magnify and to preserve behavior that would delay, if not prevent, Moroccan unification. The French and to a lesser extent the Spanish Protectorate ad-

---

[1] The most complete history of the North African tribes is undoubtedly Lloyd Cabot Briggs' *Tribes of the Sahara,* Cambridge, Harvard University Press, 1960. See also the pioneer work of Robert Montagne, *Les Berbers et le Makhzen dans le Sud du Maroc,* Paris, Alcon, 1930, and *Villages et Kasbahs Berbères,* Paris, Peyronnet et Cie., 1930. See also Jacques Berque, *Structures Sociales du Haut-Atlas,* Paris, 1955. A study devoted almost entirely to recent developments is under preparation by Ernest Gellner of the London School of Economics.

ministration also encouraged the formation of a rural elite. The French Army supported the training of young Berber officers, who were rather ironically to become the backbone of the new Royal Army officers corps, and partially prepared many Berbers for modern life through service in the enlisted ranks. These policies were by no means uniformly successful. The Berber College at Azrou, which taught no Arabic at one time, was infiltrated by the Istiqlal by the late 1940's.

The manifestations of Arab-Berber differences since independence have been intermittent and seldom organized. The nationalist struggle and the unifying role of King Mohammed V, who made frequent trips into the most remote parts of his realm, did much to create a feeling of solidarity. The first possible occasion for discontent was the merger of the Army of Liberation, which was largely made up from Rifian Berbers, with the new Royal Army, but the event was surrounded with too much patriotic fervor to permit more petty feelings. About a year and a half after independence there were increasing rumors of a rurally-based and tribally-supported party, the *Movement Populaire* (M.P.) being formed. Its development was delayed by official action, but the M.P. became one of the most important minor parties in 1959. Opposition party activity was in part inspired by resentment over the predominance of the urban elite, mostly from Fes and Casablanca, in the new government and in the Istiqlal. To these more diffuse feelings of discontent were added the discomfort, sometimes becoming misery, that the economic unification of the country entailed. In late 1958 and early 1959 nearly a million tribesman in the Taza-Rif region were involved in a surprisingly effective campaign of passive resistance, which sometimes burst out into armed warfare.[2] All these events, however, bear the mark of resentment over economic misfortune and of rural-urban differences that have been found in every political system.

The present essay, therefore, attempts to analyze the extent that differences between the two groups can be substantiated on the basis of language alone, which is, after all, the major remaining distinction. The respondents have been divided into three groups: one group (22) speaks classical Arabic in addition to Maghrebi, the second group (31) speaks

---

[2] For more details on these events, see the author's "Politics and Violence in Morocco," *Middle East Journal*, v. 13, no. 1, (Winter 1959), pp. 17-31. Drug smuggling was an important source of income for the *fellahiin* of the north.

a Berber dialect, and the third (28) indicated some knowledge of both.[3] The study does not attempt to determine if one group might be considered more or less prejudiced toward one of the other groups, but only to explore the differences among linguistic groups. Many of the differences commonly associated with racial behavior do not appear to occur in Morocco, although there are some very clear findings on the handicaps that may deter the full integration of the Berber speaking person. The linguistic difference might be most properly, and certainly most constructively, thought of as a social problem focusing on a small group of underprivileged and isolated citizens. Unfortunately there are occasional signs that some Moroccan politicians might use social differences so as to arouse the more intense feelings of racial superiority or inferiority. Nevertheless, it will be seen that the problem is similar to the national minority questions that have been successfully resolved in many political systems. The analysis suggests language differences are not an insuperable obstacle to political integration, but only the Moroccans can decide how their country will be integrated.

Of the 93 respondents, two gave no response to the language question and ten indicated that they knew only Maghrebi Arabic. The latter group is too small to be profitably analysed, but it can be described briefly to see how it compares with the other groups. On the whole the group speaking only Maghrebi Arabic seems to be more concentrated in advanced and urban areas, but only more recently involved in Istiqlal affairs. Nine of the ten persons were located in advanced provinces and five were in cities, which probably accounts for their having received more visits from the inspector than the other three groups. Although their recruitment dates are distributed among the three categories used, they generally took their present office much later (8 took office since mid-1956) than the other groups. The dates of organization are also considerably later than those given for the other groups. As might be expected they are nearly all (8) of traditional educational background and have fewer memberships than most others. However, they express

---

[3] This does not note those knowing a European language. Four persons knowing only classical also knew a European language and were included in the classical speaking group. One person who knew a Berber dialect and an European language in addition to Maghrebi Arabic was included with the bilingual group, which also includes eight persons who claimed knowledge of a European language in addition to classical Arabic and Berber.

a high degree of satisfaction with their preparation for present office (9) and for higher office (9). They might be characterized as less educated, but well integrated, highly motivated urban party officials. They are very likely typical of the lower echelon party official used to expand the Istiqlal in the advanced regions of the country.

Social Background and Language

Both the provincial and urban-rural distribution of the language groups conforms to the historic locations of the Arab and Berber speaking elements in Morocco. However, the findings also provide some important clues on how linguistic barriers are broken down. Thus, three-fourths or more of all language groups are in rural communities, but the bilingual group is most heavily concentrated in the retarded provinces, as shown in Table IV-1. This is explained in part by the islands of Berber-speaking people in some of the advanced provinces, Rabat, for example, which has put slightly more Berber speakers in advanced provinces than the generally less advanced. The effects of these two circumstances are probably beneficial. In the more privileged regions the chances of exposure to modern ways and the prevailing Arab customs is greater, thereby hastening integration of the Berber element. In the less privileged regions, the bilingual group will act as an integrating agent and serve to introduce the national language.[4]

Table IV-1

PROVINCIAL DISTRIBUTION AND LANGUAGE BY PERCENTAGE

	Classical Per Cent (N=22)	Berber Per Cent (N=31)	Both* Per Cent (N=28)
Advanced	86	61	54
Retarded	14	39	46
Chi square = .05			

* In this table and those following this language classification also includes those persons having three languages (8 cases). There were also two persons noting only a European language in addition to their Maghrebi Arabic and they have also been merged with the most skilled language group.

---

[4] The most complete study of tribal movements in Morocco is Robert Montagne's *Naissance du Proletariat Marocain*, Paris, Peyronnet, n.d., which is confined to tribal migration to Casablanca. See also André Adam," Naissance et développement d'une class moyenne," *Bulletin Economique et Social du Maroc,* v. 19, no. 68, (March 1956), pp. 489-492; and William H. Lewis, "The New Nomadism in North Africa," *The Middle East Journal,* v. 11, 1957, pp. 269-281.

An individual's ability to take party office and his general preparation for independence is influenced by the kind of personal contacts he has and the opportunities for such contacts. The number of organized groups provides some insight into the kind of social opportunities open to the linguistic groups. The classical and the bilingual groups appear to have about the same opportunity for group participation, which is interesting in the light of the higher concentration of the classical-speaking persons in the more advanced provinces. This may be accounted for by the bilingual secretaries' more effective work or superior training since their concentration in the more advanced provinces is no greater than that of the Berber-speaking secretaries. Under a third of the Berber-speaking secretaries reported more than five nationally organized groups in their area, but approximately half of both the classical and bilingual groups were in locations having five or more groups.[5] There is little doubt but that the setting of the Berber-speaking secretary is less suitable to encouraging increased group participation, and it seems that the bilingual secretary is indeed the most vigorous exponent of increased group activity in the less advanced provinces.

Table IV-2
MEMBERSHIPS AND LANGUAGE BY PERCENTAGES

	Classical Per Cent (N=22)	Berber Per Cent (N=31)	Bilingual Per Cent (N=28)
0-2	68	87	75
3 or more	32	13	25

Chi square not significant.

As might be expected, the Berber-speaking officials are less likely to join groups outside the party even where the opportunity exists. The over-all membership figures show that the classical-speaking group is the most active, with the bilingual group following and the Berber-speaking officials being the least active. The trend is not altered when provincial settings are held constant. The figures for the retarded provinces are too small to be very helpful, but in the advanced provinces roughly a third of both classical-speaking and bilingual secretaries acquire memberships at the higher rate. Among the Berber-speaking officials in advanced provinces a sixth have joined groups at the higher rate. It is interesting

---

[5] For the Berber speaking group, 9 of 31 respondents reported five or more organized groups; for the classical speaking, 11 of 22 respondents; and for the bilingual, 13 of 28. Chi square is not significant.

to note that it is the more urban classical-speaking official who is the most active in outside associations. Although the data are fragmentary, it appears that the classical-speaking official has roughly a fifty-fifty chance of joining more groups where they are found in large number, while only a fourth or less of the other linguistic groups take such opportunities.

Since written communication is limited to Arabic it is natural that the classical-speaking persons read more publications. Although Maghrebi Arabic would provide enough literary skill to read many publications, concentration of Berber-speaking officials might reasonably be expected to result in less reading on the whole. Over half of the classical group indicated that they read three or more publications, but less than a fourth of the Berber group claimed this many publications.[6] The overall finding was not affected to any great extent by provincial differences. In the advanced provinces three-fourths of the bilingual and two thirds of classical-speaking noted three or more publications, while less than a fourth of the Berber-speaking group did so. Once again it appears that the bilingual are acting as a flux in the political development of the country. Very likely they act in the role of opinion-leaders in their communities. Although the study provides no indication of how many bilingual persons are affiliated with other parties, it appears that the bilingual Istiqlal official is making an important contribution to national integration.

The restraints on the Berber-speaking group are further clarified in the comparison of language and occupation in Table IV-3. The percentage of the sample having modern occupations does not suggest that there was a heavy handicap on the Berber-speaking officials, although those with some knowledge of Arabic tend to do slightly better. The findings' broader implications are restricted because those speaking Berber and having modern occupations are probably more likely to be drawn into the Istiqlal and into political activity in general. In remote areas where Berber is more frequently used, the party may have a near monopoly of individuals with modern occupations who know a Berber dialect. The other two linguistic groups are less likely to be in remote areas and more

---

[6] For the classical speaking, 59 per cent (13 of 22 respondents) read at the level presented in the questionnaire; for the Berber speaking, 23 per cent (7 of 13), and for the bilingual, 53 per cent (15 of 28). Chi square is not significant.

likely to have varied interests outside the party. The largest differences occurs in the concentration of the Berber-speaking in traditional occupations, although the Istiqlal has apparently realized the importance of persons with modern skills regardless of language background. The nature of the occupational limitation is further clarified by the kind of modern job the linguistic groups have acquired. The Berber-speaking are officials and merchants; the bilingual are officials and modern teachers; and the classical-speaking officials include all three occupations.

Table IV-3

OCCUPATION AND LANGUAGE BY PERCENTAGES

	Classical	Berber	Both
	Per Cent (N=22)	Per Cent (N=31)	Per Cent (N=27)
Modern	41	32	40
Traditional	27	45	30
Unoccupied	32	23	30

Chi square not significant.

The comparison of educational and linguistic achievement displays the greatest variations, and it is undoubtedly in education that the persons with less linguistic skill suffer the most. Indeed, considering the proportion of the Berber-speaking secretaries who have acquired modern occupations, it appears that the Berber-speaking officials have overcome their educational limitation extremely well. Of the twenty who gave educational data only one had gone beyond the elementary level. It is also noticeable that the no responses for educational achievement are concentrated in the Berber-speaking category, which provides some rea·· son for arguing that the non-respondents are also of low educational achievement. Nearly all of the Berber-speaking in modern occupations had only an elementary education, while all the bilingual group in modern occupations (10 cases) had either secondary or university schooling, and seven of nine classical-speaking persons with modern occupations had some advanced education. This suggests that the Berber-speaking person who does acquire higher occupational status has less education, and, therefore, may find it more difficult to succeed in some areas of endeavor such as teaching.

PARTY POSITION AND LANGUAGE

The sequence of Moroccan modernization, largely determined by the proximity of the classical-speaking portions of the population to Europe, could hardly have been otherwise. It remains to be seen, however, if the party has reinforced or minimized these differences in its organization and activities. The Istiqlal's founding fathers were mostly from classical-speaking, urban groups, but their work may have contributed to reducing linguistic differentiation. A possible measure of the party's integrative effect is the extent to which those of Berber-speaking background have achieved higher office in the party, which is indicated by the sub-section and section difference. The analysis strongly supports the conclusion that language background has not been a handicap to achieving office. Two-fifths of the classical group, nearly half of the Berber group, and over half of the bilingual group were section secretaries.[7] The occurrence of the languages is, however, closely related to geography. Since the Berber-speaking official is handicapped in the more remote provinces, an analysis holding provincial setting constant would be a more rigorous measure.

The sub-groupings give a reasonable indication that there is little difference between the Berber and bilingual groups' success in achieving higher office. The bilingual have been slightly more successful in advanced provinces, another indication of their influence in the party as well as in national political integration. In the retarded provinces, where Berber may sometimes be essential, roughly a third of both Berber and bilingual groups have achieved section office. An indication of the impartiality toward, or the unimportance of, linguistic accomplishments is the findings for the classical-speaking in the advanced provinces. Even in the setting one would expect to be most favorable, these persons have not done as well as either of the groups knowing Berber. It seems fair to conclude that language has not lead to disproportionate achievement of office for any particular language group.

There is another variable that may indicate if there has been any injustice in the assignment of higher office along lines of linguistic differences. If one group has a higher proportion of its members in higher office and less experience, there are grounds to suspect unfair treatment. To examine this possibility a three variable table was made of the occupancy of previous office, present level of office and language. Among

---

[7] The histories of the party inspectors are discussed in the author's *Political Change in Morocco*, Princeton, Princeton University Press, 1961, pp. 232-234. Only one inspector had a distinctly Berber name in 1958, and he had been assigned to a southern province having a sizable Berber population.

those who have held office previously the bilingual secretaries have the best chance of achieving higher office, but the Berber-speaking group and the classical-speaking group both have about a fifty-fifty chance of becoming section secretaries. The chances of achieving higher office with no previous office are approximately the same for all language groupings. Like the previous findings, the present findings do not suggest that the Berber-speaking persons have been held back in the lower ranks of the Istiqlal and provide some reason for arguing that those with some knowledge of Berber have a better chance at section level office than those knowing only classical.

Many of the higher officials of the party have only Arabic background for historical reasons. In interviews with the party inspectors it appeared that several of them were close friends of the party's founders and only a few had Berber names. Since the inspectors are very sensitive to the taste and habits of their superiors it was thought worthwhile to see if personal contact with the inspector, as revealed in his visits, varied in any particular fashion with the party secretaries' linguistic skill. The findings show that no group had any strong advantage, although the bilingual were slightly favored. It is entirely possible, however, that the level of office will influence the number of visits made by the inspector. A three variable analysis was done to see if any linguistic group was favored at either the section or sub-section level. The results again bear out the organizational impartiality of the Istiqlal.

The findings have suggested that the Istiqlal, if it was to be truly national, had to accommodate and, to some extent, minimize linguistic differentiation. The way in which the organizational needs overcome less constructive forms of differentiation is apparent in the responses to date of recruitment. The party expanded first in the predominantly Arabic-speaking regions, which produced a larger proportion of persons knowing classical Arabic during the early phase of post-war recruitment. However, the organization soon needed persons with knowledge of Berber or with the capacity to work in the two languages. For example, nearly half of the secretaries recruited in the 1948-1954 period spoke only Berber. The emphasis was no doubt influenced by the formation of the resistance and Liberation Army during the latter part of this period.

Although it appears that allowance has been made for all linguistic groups, it is possible that the Berber-speaking secretaries have found it harder to join the party at an early age. It appears that the more isolated

Berber-speaking official was not qualified for office until age had given him the experience that his colleagues managed to acquire at an earlier age. The relationship between age, date of recruitment and language was examined in a three variable distribution. The tendency has been to recruit classical-speaking persons while they are young and Berber-speaking persons when they are older. In the early recruitment period an equal number of young and old persons having classical Arabic were recruited, while three-fourths of the Berber-speaking persons were older. The party's operation at this time, however, was certainly restricted to the areas where there were more Arabic-speaking persons. In the later period, from 1948 on, the differences are more significant since the party had the rudiments of a national organization. Youth was still favored among the classical-speaking, but most Berber-speaking officials were still recruited from older people. Thus, it appears that the less privileged Berber-speaking segment of Morocco has continued to pay a certain price for its isolation. Although members may have been recruited without regard to age and language, the local officials have tended to be older in the Berber-speaking group.

Table IV-4

DATE OF RECRUITMENT AND LANGUAGE BY PERCENTAGES

	Classical Per Cent (N=22)	Berber Per Cent (N=31)	Both Per Cent (N=26)
To 1948	45	39	42
1948-1954	27	42	35
1955 on	27	19	23

Chi square not significant.

The age disadvantage of the Berber group in reference to recruitment may not be carried over to taking office. There is some reason for allowing the less experienced member mature through age before giving him office, but it may also be that the elder Berber recruit is advanced more rapidly because of organizational needs in the more remote regions. The relationship between date of present office and date of recruitment by linguistic group has been examined in a three variable distribution. The sub-groupings are not large enough to make fast and sound generalizations but they do indicate trends that are most pertinent to the linguistic problem. Of those recruited in the early period only the bilingual appear to have taken office later, while both the classical Arabic and Berber-speaking groups had about the same chance of taking office before mid-1956. Of those recruited in the later period, the persons having some knowledge of classical, either alone or with Berber, had slightly *less* chance of taking office before mid-1956. Nearly a half of the Berber-speaking group that was recruited later took office earlier, but only about a third of the larger recruits in the other two language groups managed to take office at the earlier date. The party appears to have definitely favored the Berber-speaking group in assigning present offices, which may well have been a necessity with the recent rapid expansion in the more remote regions.

Even though the Berber-speaking person may receive equal opportunity in the party, he may find that the acquisition of experience and education takes him much longer. This may not be intentional, but simply a function of the generally less advanced state of the regions of the country in which he lives. A comparison of language and age[8] suggests that the Berber-speaking person may have needed more time to achieve the educational level of his compatriots. Two-thirds of the Berber-speaking persons were over 35 years of age, but half or less of the other two linguistic groups were over 35.

Age and aspiration reveal certain differences of interest among the linguistic groups. For both the classical-speaking and the bilingual well over half of both young and older secretaries aspired to higher office, but for the Berber-speaking there was much less evidence of the determination and confidence that contribute to aspiring to higher office. The Berber-speaking sub-groups are nearly evenly divided in their aspiration regardless of age. The elder classical and bilingual secretaries expressed the highest ambitions. If the Berber-speaking group finds itself at a disadvantage in reference to age and education, it might also be anticipated that it would carry a similar handicap in its record for holding previous office. Previous office is a useful measure of experience and success in the party. The results place the Berber-speaking group in an intermediate position, although the differences among the groups are not too large. The classical-speaking rather than the Berber-speaking seems to have had the least experience in previous office, dividing roughly in

---

[8] The most recent census is contained in the *Annuaire Statistique de la Zone Francaise du Maroc,* Rabat, Central Statistical Services, 1953, but a new census was begun in the summer of 1960. It has been estimated reliably that about half of all Moroccans are under twenty years of age, see Pierre Bertrand, "L'aspect démographique des problèmes marocains," *O.R. Marco,* no. 20, 1958, pp. 17-26.

half. Almost two-thirds of the Berber-speaking and the bilingual secretaries had previous office.[9] Thus, in one sense the Berbers have progressed more rapidly in the party organization though they were generally recruited later than the other two linguistic groups. Conversely, one might inquire why the classical-speaking secretaries who possessed the advantages of time and access have not continued to excel. The point bears more examination for it may well be that the more firmly established party officials were reluctant to share their prestige and to adapt new administrative methods.

The Berber-speaking secretary may have had a more rewarding experience and may face a more attractive future in the party than the classica-speaking official, despite the various social handicaps that the Berber-speaking person may have. Another indication of success in the party is the relation of previous office to the present level of office. At the section level, the classical-speaking secretary appears to have had a fifty-fifty chance of promotion if he previously held office while the Berber-speaking and bilingual secretary have done much better. The success of the Berber-speaking group was probably a function of the more rapid expansion of the party organization in the countryside, where local officials were more swiftly promoted regardless of experience. The classical-speaking secretary had not advanced as successfully as the other two linguistic groups despite his proximity to and familiarity with Istiqlal business.

Language differentiation seemed to be especially important in the secretaries' estimate of their preparedness for present and higher office. Once again the social disadvantage of the Berber-speaking officials is manifested, although they do not feel nearly as handicapped as their low educational record might lead one to expect. The bilingual group expressed the most confidence on both counts and the classical-speaking secretaries followed closely behind despite the rather poor record of promotion that they appear to have had. The Berber-speaking group revealed its lack of confidence in estimating preparation for higher office, although it also gave evidence of nearly as high aspirations as the other two groups. There are, of course, two possible sources of internal

---

[9] For the classical speaking, 10 of 20 respondents had previous office, while 17 of 28 Berber speaking officials and 17 of 25 bilingual officials had previous office. Chi square not significant.

party tension in these figures. The Berber-speaking secretaries appear to have expectations somewhat in excess of their qualifications by their own admission, while the classical-speaking group may not be achieving the degree of recognition that it desires.

Table IV-5

ESTIMATES OF PREPARATION FOR OFFICE AND LANGUAGE
BY PERCENTAGES OF TOTAL RESPONSES

	Classical Per Cent (N=20)	Berber Per Cent (N=25)	Both Per Cent (N=26)
Satisfactory for present office	56	46	65
Satisfactory for higher office	44	27	58

Chi square not significant.

The findings of this chapter might be summarized as indicating that within the Istiqlal the Berber-speaking group has not been as seriously mistreated as irresponsible assertions would sometimes claim. There are several respects in which the classical-speaking person has also been neglected within the party, or at least moved ahead less rapidly. These conclusions cannot, of course, be interpolated so as to apply to the entire population, but they are useful and to some extent valid in extending our knowledge of how the differentiations of language can be and are broken down in a developing nation. The Istiqlal has been forced to break down irrational considerations as the grounds of advancement in the party for the same reasons that nations encounter the same need. The party could not afford to let the segment of the population that was untouched by national politics be monopolized by other parties. Furthermore, the ultimate values of the Istiqlal demand that all persons having the interest of the nation at heart be admitted and given equal opportunity. The problem became a classic case of achievement standards overruling ascription as the party acquired a national organization.

Within the party the Berber-speaking group has been fairly treated, at least at the section and sub-section levels from which the sample comes. More of this group has attained higher office at the section level and in some respects they receive more attention from inspectors. Although they tend to have been recruited later and to be older, they have been promoted faster. The most telling evidence of their continued retardation is the low record of memberships and reading. They tend to join fewer

59

groups even where opportunities exist, although all linguistic groups appear to be poor joiners until numerous activities have been started. However, the educational handicap of the Berber-speaking officials has not held them back in the party, even though they express doubts about their preparation for higher office. In general, the Berber-speaking are aware of their handicaps as local party officials, but they still express aspirations that are nearly equal to the other two language groups.

A discovery of more general importance, and one which needs comparative study, is the nationalist party's role in the assimilation of the less modernized peoples of a new nation. Organizational analysis of the Istiqlal has shown that there are organizational hazards for a major or single party system in a rapidly developing country. Since organizational skills are generally more easily acquired and more readily understood in the more advanced portion of a new country, organizational disparities may increase, and, thereby, the advanced segment of the population may be increasingly differentiated from the retarded segment at a time when such differences might best be minimized. The findings of this inquiry provide some further insight into this problem. The Istiqlal has tended to promote the Berber-speaking officials more rapidly, and, thereby, has helped prepare some persons in the less developed parts of Morocco for modern political life. Whether the extent of this forced mobilization is sufficient to have an impact on the country's political future cannot be determined.

The crucial question is, naturally, how linguistic differentiation will play in the future of Moroccan politics. The disruptive and occasionally destructive form that it can take has been seen in India, for example, and there have been signs that it has been played on in rural Moroccan politics. It is perhaps part of the paradox of the modern nation that its successful formation requires rapid de-emphasis of irrational behavior, although the struggle for independence has stressed extreme nationalism. There is nothing to prevent Moroccans, like any other people, from associating their present, more concrete questions with the volatile, irresolvable questions of a person's supposed (in the case of the Berbers highly supposed) racial or linguistic characteristics. The tragedies of this course are manifest throughout history. One can only hope that Morocco will benefit from human experience as much or more than the advanced nations.

60

V

Nation-Building and Confidence in Office

A fundamental device in the exploration of opinions and attitudes is the comparison of what respondents think they are with what they are by external standards. When a party militant is asked to evaluate his preparation for office and his aspiration for higher office he is certainly being put under considerable cross-pressure. On the one hand, he does not want to appear disinterested, but he may also lack confidence or understand his handicaps. In the final analysis the test of sincerity is not unlike that applied in any human relationship, where the person evaluating another looks for signs that the person being judged is telling the truth. As will become apparent below, the secretaries' estimates of their preparation correlate with the kind of experience that would reasonably be expected to occur in such cases.

Systematic analysis does much more, however, than simply put our insights and crude observations into more precise and manageable form. As has become apparent from the preceding chapters, even the limited sample used here takes on additional value as the data are manipulated and compared. While this leads to some tentative hypothesis formation and the discovery of relationships that are not visible to the external observer, the benefits are multiplied when the interpretation deals with areas of human behavior of which we know very little. Indeed, an important goal of non-Western studies is to discover how familiar demographic variables help us to understand the dispositions and desires manifested by less familiar peoples.[1] The careful observer unaided with

---

[1] It is interesting to note in this regard that attitudinal studies in this country

survey data might foresee this, but intuition would not suffice in differentiating the motivations of the nationalist secretaries. Given the great lacunae in our knowledge of political behavior in developing nations, a better understanding of how individuals become involved in national politics and how they perceive their country's development is critically important.

Table V-1
ESTIMATES OF PREPARATION FOR PRESENT AND HIGHER OFFICE
(ACTUAL NUMBERS N-83)

| | | Prepared for Higher Office | |
		Yes	*No*
Prepared for	Yes	38	16
Present office	No	5	24
Chi square = .001			

The respondents have been divided into four groups possessing different estimates of their preparation for present and/or higher office as summarized in Table V - 1. Since it is desirable to explore both the general phenomenon of differences in the secretaries' confidence in their preparation as well as the relation between confidence and aspiration, the basic groupings will be briefly described and the two larger groups will be analyzed in more detail.[2]

---

indicate that sense of political efficiency, and possible other political attitudes, do not relate in a significant manner to the commonly used demographic variables. For example, see Elizabeth Donovan, "The Sense of Effectiveness and Response to Public Issues," *Journal of Social Psychology*, v. 47, 1958, pp. 114-115.

[2] The percentage breakdown for the three characteristics being analyzed in this chapter is given below. It will be noted that the comparison with the discarded cases suggests that present preparation and aspiration may diverge even more than indicated by the small sample. It may be quite possible that the findings of the chapter tend to be slightly more conservative than a larger sample would demonstrate.

| Number | Prepared for Present Office | | Prepared for Higher Office | | Aspired for Higher Office | |
	244	*93*	*244*	*93*	*244*	*93*
Yes	33%	58%	25%	46%	34%	54%
No	27	31	35	43	32	30
No response	32	11	32	11	34	16
Unscorable	8	—	8	—	—	—

There are a few factors that help clarify the background of the small group of five secretaries who felt confident of their preparation for a higher post and not confident in their present post, although they may have simply misread or misunderstood the question. In terms of their education and party histories, they are less experienced persons, although there were many other secretaries with less education and party experience who made more confident estimates of their preparation. The five secretaries gave several indications of being generally less active persons. Although the party offices where they worked were organized at a fairly early date, they did not take office until comparatively recently.

The sixteen secretaries who felt prepared for their present posts, but not for a higher post, present a similar, but more mixed picture. Nearly three-fourths (11), the highest proportion of any of the groups, are section secretaries. They appear to be fully satisfied by having gained higher level of office, which might be the limit of their ambition. The section officers divided nearly equally between those wishing and not wishing higher office, which is approximately the same distribution found among the party secretaries feeling totally unprepared. The secretaries also had strong traditional ties, and half the group had attended only traditional schools. Like the five cases, the offices of these sixteen secretaries were generally organized earlier than others, but many of the respondents did not achieve office until 1956 or later. There were few organized groups in their locations, and their membership rates were the lowest except for the five previously mentioned cases. The sixteen secretaries appear to share the background of the five least confident persons by being more remote from group activity and by having been slow to rise in the party. They have had few opportunities to distinguish themselves, although they are not an ambitious lot.

Of all the factors that might be expected to affect the secretary's estimate of his preparation for office and his aspiration for higher office, previous experience in office might be considered crucial. It provides an external check of recognition and promotion in the party. As seen in Table V-2, attaining office seems to correlate more distinctly with the secretaries' estimates of preparation for present office than for higher office. The shift that takes place in estimating preparation for higher office may be reflection of ambition exceeding party experience. Roughly two-thirds of secretaries consider themselves prepared for present or higher office if they have held previous office. However, attaining previous offices does not appear to influence the secretary if he does not feel prepared for present or higher office, i.e., in these cases there are very likely other factors entering into the official's estimate.

Table V-2
ESTIMATES OF PREPARATION, ASPIRATION AND
PREVIOUS OFFICE (ACTUAL NUMBERS)

		Prepared for Present Office (N=76)		Prepared for Higher Office (N=76)		Aspire to Higher Office (N=70)	
		Yes	No	Yes	No	Yes	No
Previous	Yes	32	12	25	19	29	13
Office	No	16	16	13	19	16	12

An analysis of the groups in Table V - 1 indicates again that the effects of previous office are substantially changed where both estimates of preparation are the same. Seventy per cent of the group feeling prepared for both higher and present office held previous office. Slightly more than forty per cent of those feeling unprepared for both higher and present office had held previous office.[3] Thus, it appears that for those feeling unprepared, attaining office does not regularly establish confidence in party participation. There are, then, additional factors at play on the secretary lacking confidence. Because of the importance of discovering how nearly independent citizens acquire the confidence that some Istiqlal secretaries expressed, these dispirited party officials are of particular interest. The problem might be imagined as that of specifying with greater accuracy the point where the newly integrated citizen, in this case the party official, begins to attach meaning to the national political system in terms of his own career and activity.

The relative advantage of the secretary in the advanced provinces produces little change in any of the self-evaluations. Roughly two-thirds of the secretaries in the advanced provinces regularly indicated more confidence, while about half of those from the retarded provinces expressed the secretaries in the advanced provinces regularly indicated more confidence, while about half of those from the retarded provinces expressed the more confident judgment consistently. It appears that the more remote, and often less well prepared, secretary may adjust his ambitions to his own estimate of preparation of office. More remote secretaries may

---

[3] For the fully confident (38), twenty-three held previous office and five gave no response. Of those having no confidence in their preparation (24), ten held previous office and one gave no response. Chi square = .01.

also depend more heavily on the party as a means of social advancement and may identify more strongly with party views. Since the party's organizational needs call for the advancement and recognition of the more talented officers, the social role of the party may sometimes conflict with internal efficiency.

Table V-3

ESTIMATES OF PREPARATION, ASPIRATION, AND
PROVINCIAL DIFFERENCES (ACTUAL NUMBERS)

	Prepared for Present Office (N=83)		*Prepared for Higher Office (N=-83)*		*Aspired to Higher Office (N=77)*	
	Yes	*No*	*Yes*	*No*	*Yes*	*No*
Advanced	41	15	34	22	37	17
Retarded	13	14	9	18	13	10

Chi square = .05, not significant, not significant, respectively.

The organizational data helps to elaborate the significance of holding of previous office. The section level of office, although not of equal significance in the eyes of the party across the nation, is more important than the sub-section level. The official's hierarchical position may be a better indicator of his present state of mind than his speculation about the future. Differences in the correlation of previous office and level of office suggest the comparative importance of the two external indicators. Surprisingly, level of office did not produce differences in the officials' self-evaluations. In relation to preparation and aspiration the respondents divided almost equally between section and sub-section officials.[4] The fact that holding higher office was not associated with more confidence in one's preparation and future in the Istiqlal indicates an important party weakness. One would reasonably expect that the expectations of nationalist party officials would vary with the success that they had had in the organization. Many of the secretaries had been members and/or officers for many years. Their failure to attach importance to the hierarchial structure of the party in terms of their past and future experience suggests that the solidarity of the nationalist party under threat may not be operative in its day to day activities.

---

[4] Section and sub-section officers expressing confidence in their preparation for present office 29 and 25 respectively; lacking confidence, 13 and 16. In the same sequence the figures for higher office were 22, 21, 20, 20, and for aspiration 26, 24, 14, 13. Chi square is not significant.

Nor do higher rates of contact with party inspectors affect the secretaries' judgments of their preparation and ambition. The secretaries may even be adversely influenced by the inspector. Those who felt adequate to both their present and higher office had less contact than those who felt unequal to present and higher posts. Subsequent inquiries may also show that the intervening organizations and associations of the person entering into national politics for the first time do indeed lack meaning. If this is the case, then the moderating and integrating effects attributed to more intricate societies may be slow to appear in developing nations.[5]

The findings concerning the secretaries' views on office and the organization of the party indicate that there are very likely other factors associated with these self-estimates. One such factor may be the immediate social environment of the local official. About a half of the fully prepared secretaries are in locations having a higher level of group development, but a third of the less confident secretaries are in an equally favorable situation. Similar results emerge from an analysis of memberships and attitude toward office. Among those feeling totally unprepared a sixth have three or more memberships, but among those feeling confident in both present and higher party positions a third have more membership outside the party. The findings suggest an hypothesis that merits further investigation. The image of the local party official as the vigorous local leader may be misleading. The confident official may not be the active, more informed person that inferences from the turbulent nationalist leaders in capital cities would indicate. The person who seeks promotion in the party may often be unprepared. He may seek office as a means of social improvement, while the prepared person may divide his time between the party and many other activities. In neither case is the party's effectiveness maximized, nor does the party become an agent for the political and social integration of the new nation.[6]

---

[5] The important distinction here is the *national* organization of new groups and associations, though this might start with regional or even communal interests as individuals begin to break out of their family-village world. From a rough approximation of how such groups may vary in different parts of a developing country see the author's "Patterns of Group Development in a New Nation," *American Political Science Review*, v. 55, no. 2, 1961, pp. 321-332.

[6] Although the comparison of aspiration, confidence of preparation and group activity is not amenable to reference group analysis, it has some related implications of importance. Thus, it seems very likely that those secretaries who feel less confident and who are less active in groups may have what S. N. Eisenstadt has called

The demographic variables of age, language, education and occupation bear out the organizational factors limiting the party's usefulness as a political device as well as an integrating force. Approximately half of those persons with a Koranic education feel prepared for present or higher office, and slightly more than half aspire to higher office. While those with secondary or university education are extremely confident of their preparation, they are less likely to aspire to higher office. Nearly all the respondents having secondary education felt prepared for their present office, and two-thirds aspired to higher office.[7] Of the ten respondents with university education that gave replies, eight considered themselves prepared for present and higher office and seven aspired to higher office.

The over-all figures establish that advanced education contributes immeasurably to confidence in party office, but education does not necessarily bring a change in aspiration of the same magnitude. The educated local party official may also develop more outside interests and be less satisfied with the kind of rewards that the Istiqlal offers. Conversely, the less educated secretary may feel much less confident in a responsible party role, but may have higher aspirations.

The conflict is magnified in an analysis of provincial differences and elementary education. Of the forty-three persons having an elementary education and living in advanced provinces, about two-thirds feel prepared for their present office and aspire to higher office. Of those in retarded provinces with elementary education less than a third feel prepared for present or higher office, but three-fourths aspire to higher office. The place where the Istiqlal is most likely to encounter the ambitious and unprepared secretary is in the more remote countryside, where persons are more likely to be looking for relief and escape from difficult circumstances. The Istiqlal's failure in the remote provinces has been born out with the emergence of the Popular Movement, a tribal party, and more recently a party oriented to the monarchy having strong rural appeal.

---

a "closed status image," i.e., those persons more likely to judge themselves and their social position by affective relationships and cultural goals. See his "Reference Group Behavior and Social Integration: an Explorative Study," *American Sociological Review*, v. 19, no. 2 (April 1954), p. 180.

[7] Of the 40 respondents with elementary education, 21 felt prepared for their present office, 17 felt prepared for higher office, and 25 aspired to higher office. Of the 22 officials with secondary education, the same figures are 21, 15, and 14.

The secretaries' judgments are also strongly influenced by occupation, and in a manner very similar to education. About two-thirds of those in modern occupations and the unoccupied are confident of their preparation for present and higher office, and approximately two-thirds of the two occupational groups also aspired to higher office. Those in traditional occupations varied between their estimates of preparation and aspiration in much the same way as those having elementary education. Of the thirty respondents having traditional occupations, about a third considered themselves prepared for present office and for higher office, but more than half indicated their desire for higher office. The Istiqlal is confronted with expectations and desires from the less skilled that are more numerous and more desperate than the demands from the more skilled. These factors multiply the problems of the nationalist transition at the local level and seriously limit the party's ability to transform itself into a more specialized, effective organization in the independence period.

Table V-4

ESTIMATES OF PREPARATION, ASPIRATION, AND OCCUPATION
(ACTUAL NUMBERS)

	Prepared for Present Office (N=82)		Prepared for Higher Office (N=82)		Aspired to Higher Office (N=77)	
	Yes	*No*	*Yes*	*No*	*Yes*	*No*
Modern	22	6	17	11	19	9
Traditional	12	18	9	21	15	11
Unoccupied	19	5	16	8	16	7

Chi squares = .001, .001, not significant, respectively.

The detailed differences in the confidence estimates and occupations elaborate the social transformation that contributes to self-reliance in political life. Minor officials who have some official prestige bestowed on them by virtue of their work, expressed more confidence and higher aspirations than the merchants. Ten of the fourteen minor officials considered themselves prepared for present and higher office, but only one of the eight merchants felt equally confident. Eight of the minor officials admitted aspiring to higher office and feeling qualified for higher office. None of the merchants aspired to greater party recognition and seven indicated that they were not prepared for higher office. Although these quantities are small, they suggest that there may be important attitudinal shifts among persons participating in more advanced occupations. The nature of this attitudinal expansion associated with social advancement is certainly a key element in creating confidence in political roles.

The analysis of the Istiqlal officials indicates that party experience in a developing nation does not necessarily compensate for lack of skill when dealing with questions of increased political and social activity. The notion that a new country can move ahead more rapidly as political organizations promote mobility and spread information may be misleading. The desirable social effects may precede political confidence. Political development may depend to a large extent on the specializations and communications monopolized by the central government alone. The ground for pessimism is the extent to which experience in the Istiqlal, as denoted by previous office, has little relation to establishing confidence in office for persons in the traditional occupational category.

Age correlations showed especially clear trends when compared to attitude toward office, although the trends may be partly accounted for by youth's unavoidable claim to higher educational and modern occupational achievement. The available figures leave little doubt that increasing age is associated with decreasing aspirations and confidence in preparation. This may be a passing phenomenon in the sense that it has been created by the rapid social adjustment that Morocco and similar countries have attempted, but it is nevertheless an important factor in estimating political developments in the future. Although there has been general agreement on the importance of youth, especially of young college students, in the developing nations, very little precise knowledge yet exists on what characteristics predominate among other categories of active, young political participants.

The over-all trends are displayed in the evaluations expressed in Table V - 5. The young persons were much more likely to feel prepared for party office than their elders. Indeed, the elder officials are most likely not to feel prepared for higher office, although their aspirations compare with young officials. The older persons may not lower his aspirations despite his lower confidence in his preparation for office. This is, of course, another example of the organizational conflict that the Istiqlal and other nationalist parties may encounter. The problem may be even more serious than is apparent in this sampling since the older people very likely predominate in the party cadre, and enjoy considerable local prestige in most rural communities.

Table V-5
ESTIMATES OF PREPARATION, ASPIRATION AND AGE
(ACTUAL NUMBERS)

	Prepared for Present Office (N=81)		Prepared for Higher Office (N=81)		Aspiration for Higher Office (N=75)	
	Yes	No	Yes	No	Yes	No
35 years and under	33	8	27	14	25	14
Over 35 years	20	20	15	25	24	12

Chi squares = .01, .02, not significant, respectively.

There are two principle hypotheses that emerge from the findings of this chapter. They require further examinations as more survey work is done among the less advanced members of new nations. First, there seems to be a critical phase in individual political mobilization in the development of a national political system. The growth of a national political awareness and confidence in national political activity seems to conform to the time-worn maxim that "nothing succeeds like success." Persons who had begun to establish confidence and high aspirations had acquired some of the external, social indicators of success. But those who lacked confidence or aspiration did not seem to derive psychological compensation from experience or success in the party. The roll of the nationalist party as a socializing or politicizing agent on the national level may be easily exaggerated. Conversely, the local militant of a national party may continue to feel constraints and apprehensions when viewing national politics even after significant political achievement.

On the more optimistic side, expectations seem to rise rapidly once the secretary establishes a minimum of confidence in his ability and his future. For example, length of party association did not produce important differences in the self-estimates of preparation and aspiration, but occupation and education did. At some point in the official's development there was a dramatic re-structing of his attitudes toward national politics and his willingness to attach his personal life to national affairs. Although being in a nationalist party does not mean that one's personality is necessarily "nationalized," it appears that a fairly sudden and encompassing shift is made. A better understanding of this metamorphosis is essential to our knowledge of the nation-building process.

Another area of speculation is elaborated by the findings on the levels of group development and levels of membership. The concept of the nationalist movement as an integrator of the new society and as a vehicle for social mobility may need revision. The Istiqlal, like the major parties found in many developing nations, may be persuasive, but unable to make important contributions to its militants' well-being. The persons who feel themselves and their futures more closely associated with the party, at least as indicated by expressions of confidence and aspiration vis-à-vis the party, are in remote, less articulated social settings. Moreover, as the local official gains in experience and worldly knowledge his ties to the party appear to weaken. The decreasing importance of the party may not be so much that the party means less to him in any absolute sense, but that other activities come to mean more to him. Social advancement may mean that national political organizations are temporarily weakened. In the development of more specialized and more complex political systems in the new nations this transition may be a crucial one, and is undoubtedly closely related to the new nation's capacity to support and foster a more intricate, complex social system.

The immediate organizational problems of the Istiqlal were apparent in the comparison of the demographic variables and the self-evaluations. The more highly educated official was well aware of his superior preparation for office, but his level of aspiration was no greater than the less educated. In the remote provinces, where the Istiqlal has been weak and needs a better organization, the problem becomes even more acute. Similar trends were established in the analysis of occupation. Age differences also reveal grounds for pessimism. Among the young persons, who are generally more influential, there is undoubtedly more confidence in office, but proportionately less ambition for higher office than expressed by elder secretaries. Although there is still much more to be learned about the acquisition of confidence and ambition in an emergent political system, these preliminary findings suggest that even the experienced and respected nationalist party may have difficulty in generating the attitudes conducive to organizational effectiveness and party discipline. The Istiqlal's shortcomings may have very likely contributed to the party's split in early 1959.

VI

Religious Decompression in Political Life

Probably no aspect of Islamic affairs has been the subject of more speculation and scholarly concentration than religion. The history of the Arab world and much of the non-Arab world can be written in terms of the expansion of Islam. There are many signs that Islam has great appeal to the underdeveloped nations. Islam is one of the most frequently cited common factors in Arab politics and an important factor in the internal affairs of many underdeveloped countries peripheral to the Arab world. While its presence cannot be denied, there has been relatively little speculation concerning its precise relation to political behavior.[1] The difficulty in attaching political meaning to Islamic beliefs is not unique with this religion. Whether viewed as a set of ultimate values or social obligations, religious beliefs are difficult to relate to political life. There are, nevertheless, certain reasons that make Islam an especially attractive subject for such speculation. It is a pervasive and encompassing religion. Even the most modern citizens of a new Muslim nation find it difficult to ignore their religion. There are many who continue to use it as a political rallying cry and, with less success, as a panacea.

Many of the earlier scholarly inquiries are concerned more with the

---

[1] When traditional scholars make such interpretations they generally focus on ideological relationships which are sometimes hard to relate to behavior under specific conditions. An interesting and thought-provoking example is Bernard Lewis's "Communism and Islam," in Ruth N. Anshen, *Mid-East: World Center Yesterday Today and Tomorrow*, New York, Harpers, 1956, pp. 305-315. (Reprinted from *International Affairs*, v. 30, no. 1, January 1954).

theological and philosophical aspects of Islam than with its behavioral content or political meaning in the modern world. Nearly all previous study has proceeded from the general to the particular, the assumption being that the understanding of values, their origin and their transformation, tells a little about every Muslim. This is not too helpful when we wish to understand contemporary Muslims acting in an extremely complex and partially understood modern world. A good deal has been done to explain the behavior of the extremist Muslims.[2] In the case of the fanatical sects and brotherhoods, however, we are indeed considering some of the rare instances where prediction is greatly facilitated because individuals permit their actions be dictated solely by their religious conscience. In some instances the behavior that is stimulated has resulted in such complete rejection of world affairs that normal life would come to an end were there not less pious persons available to provide sustenance for the fanatical. There is little doubt but that a modern nation cannot be run successfully under such circumstances, and that the kind of Muslim to be found most frequently in the new nation is not totally committed to his religion any more than most members of other religious denominations in other countries.

The present chapter, then, may not be recognizable to the conventional students of Islam as a study of religion. It proceeds by different methods and seeks to illuminate a different problem. The problem of this chapter will be to see how, if at all, the Istiqlal militants have been affected in their party roles, in their general background, and in their opinions according to self-estimates of their religious fervency. One of the questions asked the secretary to indicate whether he considered himself a fervent, moderate, disinterested or disbelieving (agnostic or aetheist) Muslim. Because the subject is controversial and delicate, it was expected that the response would be very poor. In fact all but eight of the small sample gave a self-estimate, which includes forty-two fervent, forty-five moderate, one disinterested and two deviate Muslims. The latter three persons were included with the moderately religious to

---

[2] For example, see Freeland Abbott, "The Jama' at-i-Islami of Pakistan," *Middle East Journal*, v. 11, Autumn 1957, pp. 37-51, and Khalid Bin Sayeed, "The Jama' at-i-Islami Movement in Pakistan," *Pacific Affairs*, v. 30, March 1957, pp. 59-68. Inquiries of this kind are difficult to relate in a reliable manner to the political system as a whole, even though they may be of crucial importance in short run situations.

provide two groupings, which will be referred to as the religious and the less religious.[3]

Unfortunately the data do not permit taking the inquiry one step further and seeing to what extent the persons in either one of the religious groupings actually perform similar religious behavior. Several questions were included to elicit information about observance of rituals and obligations posed by Islam, but the response could not be regarded as having comparable significance. Attendance at the mosque, for example, may vary regardless of religious belief because isolated villages cannot afford to build mosques. There are many reasons, however, that suggest that it is important to have the subjective judgement, even without external checks, in the study of national political development. Even when accompanied with certain externally observable evidence of devotion, we have no grounds yet for estimating how a given degree of religious belief leads to any particular kind of political behavior. Assuming that the external check correlated with religious self-estimates we would still have no grounds for predicting the political correlates, if any, of such data. Speculation would still be confined to the religious realm. The interest of this study is to project our knowledge of religious belief into political affairs.

The great importance of Islam in the Istiqlal's development also justifies exploration of the religious self-estimates. In its very early days the Moroccan nationalist movement was inspired by religious reformers and placed very strong emphasis on the preservation of Islam in Morocco. The party's first leaders, who still lead the Istiqlal after the 1959 schism, were drawn into politics by French moves to retard the spread of orthodox Islam in the more remote regions of the country. Allal Al-Fassi and his students at Qarawiyn university were the core of the early nationalist agitation in Fes, and his thinking is still influential in Morocco. The early period of the party's development underscored religious piety and

---

[3] Compared to the discarded responses, the small sample favors the less religious, and has also virtually eliminated no responses:

	Discarded Sample (N = 244)	Analysis Sample (N = 93)
No response	28%	3%
Fervent	41	45
Moderate	29	48
Unbelievers	2	3

devotion, and these values are still highly regarded in the party and in the country as a whole.[4]

The regional and urban-rural structure of the two groupings generally confirms expectations as to the effect of living under more modern circumstances.[5] Nearly two-thirds of the more religious persons were located in advanced provinces, while almost three-fourths of the less religious were in advanced provinces. The failure of the more traditional setting to produce religious differences may be partly accounted for by the close association between the party and orthodox Islam. Throughout the country the party has very likely recruited its local officials from among those particularly influenced by Islam and its reform. Those embracing Islam in the more remote locations might even be encouraged to give it more emphasis. There are social forces at work in both the advanced and the retarded settings that work to reduce religious differences.

The provincial distribution of the religious and less religious persons also indicates that party officials have approximately the same overall religious impact throughout the country. However, this does not give us an indication of the fate of party officials within the party in respect to their religious feeling. The Istiqlal may be experienced in working among many kinds of persons, but the higher party officials are no doubt sensitive to their subordinate's religious feelings and place great value on devotion to Islam. For this reason it is important to see how religious feeling may have affected the local officials' advancement and responsibilities in the party. The overall figures according to level of office suggest that religious feeling has made little difference in the acquisition of office at higher levels of responsibility in the party.[6] There is some

---

[4] At an early phase of the nationalist development the requirement of discipline and sacrifice may be so great that the new party may use religious forms that it actually disapproves in order to organize support. There is some evidence that the Istiqlal supporters tried to use rural sections in parts of Morocco, and some claims that new sects were encouraged of "Allyines" after the leader of the Istiqlal, Allal Al-Fassi. See Robert Rezette, *Les Partis Politiques Marocaines,"* Paris, Armand Colin, pp. 23-27 and 281-284.

[5] In the advanced provinces 27 of 62 respondents estimated themselves to be fervent Muslims; in the retarded provinces 15 of 28 were fervent. Chi square is not significant.

[6] Of the more religious persons, 21 were section officers and 21 were sub-section officers; of the less religious 20 were section officers and 28 sub-section officers. Chi square is not significant.

evidence to suggest that the more religious persons had slightly greater chances of reaching section level office, but this might be easily accounted for by their higher motivation in other respects.

Although the available data indicates that religious feeling has no great importance in the organizational structure of the party, it is entirely possible that it had more effect at an earlier time. The religious influences on the Moroccan nationalists are well known, and Islam has often served to mobilize political strength. Date of office is an important indicator of actual responsibility being given to a person with known religious sentiment. The less religious were more numerous among those taking office at an earlier date, although the results must be qualified by the errors of recall and also the fact that a long time span is involved. Even with reservations the findings suggest that the local levels of the party were not dominated as much as might have been expected by more devout religious persons. The more religious persons seem to have come into the party in larger numbers in 1956, when the major internal reorganization of the Istiqlal took place. The more religious have continued to be important since that time. What may be happening is that the more religious person began to acquire offices in 1956, while the older organizations were handled by the less religious. This would be consistent with the likelihood that the more religious person is generally a less qualified official, which other evidence substantiates.

Since the date of office is an important indicator of earlier recognition within the party framework several additional analyses were done to see how the achievement of office might be related to other factors. The most important of these relates to provincial locations. Taking the less religious first, they appear to have come from advanced provinces in roughly a two to one ratio regardless of date of office. However, the less consistent advancement of the more religious party secretaries is very noticeable. In the pre-1956 period they were apparently less numerous than the less religious secretaries. In the retarded provinces the more religious acquired office in large numbers in 1956. The trend seems to have reversed in the post-1956 period, when both religious types took office at roughly the same rate in both advanced and retarded provinces. The overall effect was to make the more religious official proportionately as numerous in retarded provinces in 1956, and in the advanced provinces in the post-1956 period.

The less religious person on the whole seems to have been important in the party organization for a longer time and sometimes reached important positions sooner than the more religious official. The difference has even more significance because both kinds of officials seem to have been recruited at about the same rate.[7] Before 1948 when the religious stress was greatest, the party recruited about the same proportion of future officials from both religious groups. When organization became more difficult because of colonial opposition and the party began to operate in a more varied setting and over longer distances in the 1948-1954 period, less religious officials were nearly twice as common. In the most recent period, when the Istiqlal had to operate in competition with other parties and when there were many opportunities for talented local citizens, the religiously oriented local officials again became equally numerous.

The findings follow the known historical needs of the party, although more recent trends are not entirely clear. If it is correct that the Istiqlal has had to rely more heavily on the more religious persons since independence the internal strains that contributed to the split are more easily understood. If the patry has had to give more recognition to the claims of the more religious local leaders in national politics, the more secular leaders of the U.N.F. P. faction may have indeed felt threatened in 1958. It is also important to note that although the same numbers of both religious and less religious persons were being admitted to the party at an early time, the less religious were more successful in acquiring office and may have made a larger contribution in the pre-independence period. The relative handicap that the more fervent local official seems to have had in getting into office cannot be explained by his not being present in the party ranks. He was recruited about as often in the early period, but was not likely to take office until 1956 and even then was more likely to advance in places the party had more recently organized.

The disadvantage of the more religious person is confirmed and clarified in an analysis of the level of office and date of recruitment. Once again the sub-groupings are small, but the trends are valuable in explaining the role of the religiously motivated person in a nationalist

---

[7] Of the religious secretaries 44 per cent (18) were recruited before 1948; 24 per cent (10) from 1948 to 1954; and 32 per cent (13) after 1954. The same figures for the less religious are 40 per cent (19), 40 per cent (19), and 19 per cent (9). Chi square is not significant.

movement. The findings indicate where the two types of secretaries now rest in the party hierarchy in respect to time in the growth of the Istiqlal. For example, although nearly the same number of religious and less religious party officials were recruited before 1948, the religious official recruited at that time has had a two to one chance of becoming a section secretary, but the chances were two to one against the less religious official acquiring section office. The balance shifted in the 1948 to 1954 period, when the less religious secretary came into the party in larger numbers and also had about an equal chance of rising to higher party office. Since 1954 the trend has been reversed, although the more religious secretary is more numerous. The more religious person had about one chance in three of becoming a section secretary, and the less religious still about an even chance of being promoted. The more religious person brought into the party at an early time was generally better qualified for office and better suited to the party's problems of the moment than those recruited more recently. The possibility of tension arising that might lead to internal party conflict is suggested by their being roughly equal numbers of secretaries of each religious sentiment as of 1958.

These speculations are supported by the evidence of a comparison of education, date of recruitment and religious sentiment. The more religious secretaries recruited in the earliest period were divided nearly equally between Koranic and more advanced schools. Those recruited in the most recent period are predominately from the Koranic schools. The less religious secretaries, in contrast, have been approximately evenly divided between elementary and more advanced education for each recruitment period. Although previous inquiry has shown that the Istiqlal organization may not have been sensitive to educational experience, it appears that the Istiqlal's initial religious appeal attracted well prepared religious persons. More recent developments have attracted more persons with less religious sentiment and having better education, while the more recently recruited person of stronger religious sentiments tends to be less well prepared. The dilemma of the party is considerable for in effect it has had to accommodate officials with more religious sensitivities and less preparation as the country as a whole advanced and party competition grew.

The data on organizational and social participation have on the whole supported the conclusion that the religious orientation of persons in positions of similar responsibility and having similar historical experience does not significantly vary. Although there are indications that persons of a particular religious type were recruited or promoted in large numbers in some periods, these differences seem to have equaled out over time. Party experience, of course, subjected all the officials to a common orientation, but the secretaries may still be persons having very different backgrounds in other respects. The demographic variables provided means for testing this hypothesis.

The educational similarity is especially surprising, for it has often been asserted that modern or traditional education had a peculiar relationship to religious behavior. Rather like the opposition to progressive education among fundamentalist Christians there has been some feeling among Muslims that advanced education drew persons away from religion. The following table shows slight tendencies in this direction, but the differences are hardly great enough to justify either position.

Table VI-1
EDUCATION AND RELIGIOUS SELF-ESTIMATES BY PERCENTAGES

	Religious Per Cent (N=34)	Less Religious Per Cent (N=42)
Elementary	56	52
Secondary	26	33
University	18	14

Chi square = not significant.

The religious character of the Koranic schools has often been assumed to reinforce religious sentiments. There is no evidence of this here, although it should be acknowledged that educational effects might be removed through party indoctrination. There are indications of less religious feeling among those with secondary education, who are likely to be most conscious of their social progress and most eager to display the alleged attributes of social advancement. It is noteworthy that so many of the best informed and most articulate local leaders continue to value their religion so highly despite the distractions and temptations that accompany their educational advancement.

Table VI-2 reveals several thought-provoking characteristics of the secretaries' religious feelings even with allowance made for their fairly homogeneous political background. The trends indicate that the religious self-evaluations are not purely chance phenomena. Although youth are often less religious, the move away from religious interest is not over-

80

whelming. Elder party officials are more religious, but about a third judge themselves less religious. While the elders may rely more heavily on Islam the youngsters do not seem to be drawn away from it to an alarming degree nor to a degree that is frequently asserted by traditional Moroccan politicians. The findings support the commonly heard assertion that Morocco remains a very religious country.

Table VI-2
AGE AND RELIGIOUS SELF-ESTIMATES BY PERCENTAGES

	Religious Per Cent (N=41)	Less Religious Per Cent (N=47)
Less than 30 years	22	38
30-40	32	47
Over 40	46	15
Chi Square = .01		

The results of the comparison of language and religious sentiment run counter to the frequently used argument that the scholar of classical Arabic, being proficient in the language of the religion, is more likely to be religious. Using the totals of those knowing classical Arabic, a Berber dialect, or the bilingual group, is probably the most severe test of how language facility may relate to religious feeling. The religious and less religious are equally distributed for each of the language groups. A comparison of age, language, and religious feeling showed that for the secretary knowing only one language, either classical Arabic or a Berber dialect, age and religious feeling were not too important. For persons knowing both languages, however, age and religion display interesting variations. Most of the bilingual secretaries over thirty-five years of age (11 of 15) were more religious and most of the secretaries under thirty-five (13 of 17) were less religious. These findings support the same trends revealed with the organizational data. The overall development of the country, and the generational changes inherent in such change, has unavoidable secular effects. The Istiqlal can maintain its relative homogeneity in Islamic affairs only at a certain price in organizational efficiency and appeal to more secular groups.

The religious groups have similar aspirations toward higher office, although there are considerable differences in their party experience. Approximately three-fifths of both groups indicated that they aspired to higher office.[8] Remembering that the sample is entirely of Istiqlal background, the failure of the groups to differ in aspiration is of special interest. It suggests that a variety of sentiments may be subdued by a minimum of party indoctrination and familiarity with national politics. The officials appear to orient their behavior to party goals regardless of their religious sentiment. The new citizen may rapidly shed religious restraint at least in so far as such restraints might keep him from aspiring to greater recognition and office in the emerging political system.

The findings on aspiration are very different from the externally observable record of party accomplishments as denoted by holding previous office. The less religious party secretary is much more likely to have had previous party office. The findings help interpret the meaning of the nearly undifferentiated results of the question on aspiration to higher office. The more religious person seems to be relatively unaffected by holding previous office in making his judgement as to aspiration to higher office. The less religious person, on the contrary, has a better record of holding previous office, but he aspires to office no more frequently than the religious secretary. The implications are contrary to expectations, which would suggest that the less religious, more experienced and higher aspiring characteristics should converge.

Table VI-3
PREVIOUS OFFICE AND RELIGIOUS SELF-ESTIMATES
BY PERCENTAGES

	Religious Per Cent (N=38)	Less Religious Per Cent (N=44)
Yes	47	70
No	53	30

Chi square = .05

In a comparison of aspiration, office holding and religious feeling, it appears that the religious secretary with no previous office and the less religious secretary with previous office aspired to higher office in two cases out of three. However, the religious secretary with previous office and the less religious secretary with no previous office had much less ambitious hopes for advancement in the party. This is in harmony with our general knowledge of the Istiqlal and previous findings. The

---

[8] Of the more religious, 61 per cent (22 of 36 respondents) aspired to higher office; of the less religious 59 per cent (27 of 46). Chi square is not significant.

less experienced religious person may look to the Istiqlal as an avenue of self-improvement and the more experienced may be content with the prestige and advancement already achieved. The aspiration analysis provides additional evidence of the kind of problem the Istiqlal may encounter when trying to advance more religious persons in the party hierarchy.

The characteristics of those secretaries feeling confident of their preparation for their present offices helps clarify how political experience relates to religious feelings. About half of the religious and nearly three-fourths of the less religious felt prepared for their present office.[9] The difference is large enough to suggest that the religious person may be under a psychological handicap exceeding his real handicap of less experience. Holding preparation for office constant, it appears that the religious secretary who feels prepared has actually attained office previously much less frequently than the less religious secretary. Having held office does not appear to raise the more religious secretaries' self-estimates as much as the estimates of the less religious.

The secretaries' failure to express more pronounced differences on the basis of their religious differentiation was tested in several ways because religious feeling is so frequently assumed to be of great influence in the political affairs in the Muslim countries. Religion may loom up on a grand scale at the national level where leaders tend to seek religious values to reinforce decisions and where religion may be used to create a rather fragile kind of political integration. Our historical and theological interest in the Muslims may have predisposed our thinking to a greater extent than has been realized. The results of the exploration suggest that in the work-day world a Muslim with a degree of political experience, such as the Istiqlal party official, does not rely very heavily on his religion in order to orient himself to political and social problems in the real world.[10] It might be objected that despite such a demonstra-

---

[9] Of the more religious 54 per cent (20 of 37 respondents) felt prepared for their present offices, and of the less religious (31 of 34) felt prepared. Chi square = .10.

[10] There is some collaborative evidence that religious differences are of little significance among more specialized Muslims. In Morroe Berger's study of Egyptian civil servants, *Bureaucracy and Society in Modern Egypt*, p. 64, it appears that the Muslim-Copt differences did not correlate in a meaningful way with the various indices being applied. Much more work could be done along the lines suggested in the study of religion in American politics, where it appears that the Catholic vote has less importance as Catholic groups are assimilated socially and develop

tion most Muslims are not experienced and articulate in the political realm. The objection is precisely what needs to be elicited in order to construct an explicit, empirical basis by which the significance of religion in various developing countries can be compared. To make the grounds of comparison clear and to encourage comparative inquiry in Middle Eastern and other cross-national studies is precisely what is needed.[11]

The precise meaning of the findings on religion bear some clarification. The results of this chapter and the corroborative studies that have been noted do not signify that religion will cease to have value in the lives of Moroccans and other Muslim peoples. Nor is it suggested that Islam cannot continue to make important contributions in the political realm of nations developing with predominantly Islamic backgrounds. There is, however, increasing evidence that the contemporary Muslim thinks about political problems in a way similar to Westerners as the Muslim world modernizes. Religious values come to be of less value in orienting one's self to political and social issues by virtue of knowing more about such issues and recognizing the intricacy of the more advanced society.[12] The pervasive influence of the religion is reduced, but this does not mean that it sacrifices the moral value and personal significance that religion has had in the lives of all peoples.

The fragmentary evidence that this study compiles is of even greater suggestiveness in showing how important national leadership may be in the conversion of the religious role. National organizations like the

a variety of interests. See Angus Campbell, et. al., *The American Voter, op. cit.*, pp. 295-332.

[11] There have been several attitudinal studies that help specify the importance of religious values and religious meaning in political and social problems. In the following articles religious differences were not significant. E. Terry Prothro and Levon Melikian, "Social Distance and Social Change in the Near East," *Sociology and Social Research*, v. 37, no. 1, (October 1952), pp. 3-11. Levon H. Melikian and Lufty N. Diab, "Group Affiliations of University Students in the Arab Middle East," *Journal of Social Psychology*, v. 49, 1959, pp. 145-159. Douglas E. Ashford, "The Political Usage of 'Islam' and 'Arab Culture,'" *The Public Opinion Quarterly*, v. 25, no. 1, (Spring 1961) pp. 106-114.

[12] There have been few attempts to sort out the changing role of ultimate values during the transition to more advanced social forms. Some of the best experimentation has been done in Israel, where there is indeed a range of social advancement represented by refugees from countries of different stages of advancement. See S. N. Eisenstadt, "Communication Systems and Social Structure: An Exploratory Comparative Study," *Public Opinion Quarterly*, v. 19, 1955, pp. 153-167.

Istiqlal bring together mixes of personal sentiment about religion. To a large extent the leader decides whether or not to rely on the emotional power of the religion to perserve political solidarity and to solve new problems. The shortcomings of the highly affective appeal in the face of pressing and complex concrete difficulties are well known, and it is no doubt significant that the trend throughout the Muslim world over the past generation has been to rely less and less on Islam for detailed solutions to social problems arising from modernization.

Although much more empirically oriented research is needed on the role of religion in political development, the available data have also exposed some of the potential points of conflict. For example, in the retarded provinces religious sentiment seems to vary little with age, while in the more advanced provinces religious differences separate old and young more sharply. From the Istiqlal's viewpoint there are additional problems created by the tendency of the less privileged feeling stronger ties to the religion to ignore the importance of experience in the party as a criteria for advancement in party office and as a basis for evaluating their own role in the party. In contrast it should be noted that the more religious person having a long party history, and probably sharing some of the prestige of being an historic party militant of the region, is more able to differentiate his religious feelings from the needs of the party. Indeed, his ability to do so demonstrates in another way the crucial role of leadership in helping the more recently recruited party militants to distinguish political and religious roles. The fact that some deeply religious persons come into the party's ranks means that the Istiqlal can act either to reinforce convictions as total solutions to the challenge of modernization, or it can contribute to the articulation of religious sentiments in a way that will facilitate the creation of a more intricate society.

The evidence also suggests that there may be a critical phase in the attitudinal development of the emerging local leader. The pattern of aspiration and also educational differences among the more religious reveal a remarkable shift in attitudes toward religion in public affairs. The Muslim leaders should derive some assurance from the fact that Moroccans have been able to advance in the party organization and undergo an extended period of social transformation while preserving their religious faith. For the more privileged party militant, advancing in the party and involvement in modern political activity has not meant discarding Islam. The qualification that must be made, however, is that these persons very likely place less strenuous demands on the party. Their ability to relate their experience to party needs indicates a degree of cognitive advancement which relieves the party of the need to provide social rewards and personal security.

VII

Removing the Aftermath of Violence

All the North African countries have encountered serious problems in absorbing the participants of the national resistance movements. Algeria will require many years to erase the tragic effects of the revolution, which has touched nearly every household. In Tunisia there was a bitter quarrel between President Bourguiba and Salah Ben Youssef, who had the support of resistance remnants in the south. The more profound social significance of Tunisian differences are revealed in the echos of the controversy in the 1963 attempt on Bourguiba's life, which was motivated in part by discontented resistance elements. The resistance organization in Morocco was much larger than the Tunisian, though it never reached the scale of the Algerian Revolutionary Army. However, it did have distinct rural orgins as well as an urban terrorist element. With independence, groups of terrorists split off according to earlier political alignments and the wishes of their leaders,[1] but the solidarity of the struggle lingers on and there remains a royally sponsored Council of the Resistance to ease the adjustment of the Moroccan resistance fighter to peaceful life.

The survey established the party officials' role, if any, in the 1952-1955 movement. Thus, the chapter cannot be properly classified as a study of the attitude toward violence in a going political system, fascinating as this might be. The focus is rather on how participation in violent

---

[1] For a more complete description of events during this period and their after-math in Moroccan political affairs see the author's "Politics and Violence in Morocco," *Middle East Journal*, v. 13, no. 1, Winter Issue 1959, pp. 17-31.

activity in an independence struggle may have affected political views in the new nation. The data cannot tell us whether or not the respondents presently approve or disapprove of violence in any particular context, but does testify to their willingness to engage in violence on behalf of their country. It is entirely possible, of course, that many secretaries who never participated in the Moroccan resistance were never presented with opportunities to do so. For this reason, the following analysis concentrates on how such participation seems to relate to the officials careers in the party and to their own qualifications and background.

Moroccans are extremely reluctant to discuss the resistance organization among outsiders. Although it has gone through several transformations since the years of widespread terrorism, the resistance organization was still largely clandestine in 1958. Through the National Council of unknown membership, its political influence was exercised discreetly. The members of the present resistance groups, or even those persons who had participated and have since drifted away, would probably not have replied to queries on their terrorist background without the assurance that the Istiqlal endorsement provided. It should also be stated clearly that the resistance has not taken a uniform view on the emergence of parties. For these reasons generalizations as to the effects of participation in terrorist or even less bloody resistance activity must be made with caution.

The justification of the present inquiry rests elsewhere. Seldom have we been able to examine as systematically a variety of information about persons who were drawn into the most active phase of an independence struggle. In the politics of developing nations violence often plays a large role, and it is a form of political expression that is almost unheard of in the more highly developed political systems. In the advanced nations violence is generally expressed in very personal situations or in the more remote conflicts of war. Violence seldom plays an intermediate role, nor do we concern ourselves excessively with how it may play in everyday politics. This is not the case in the developing nations and it behooves the social scientist, and possibly more reluctantly the diplomat, to give some attention as to how this experience may affect the internal politics of the newly emerging countries. One of the first hurdles of the new nation wishing to establish an effective viable government is the elimination of violence as a widespread form of political expression. For these reasons the following examination of the characteristics of resistance participants, and their differences from the non-participants, will focus on how the resistance veterans seem to have then assimilated in the new political system.

The breakdown of the available cases according to their resistance background was especially fortuitous in several respects. The total sample of 93 included only 8 persons who gave no response.[2] Of the 85 remaining respondents approximately half, 46, indicated that they had not participated; about a third, 26, indicated that they had been in both the rural resistance organization, the Army of Liberation, and the urban resistance; and the remainder, 13, were in the Army of Liberation only. In the preliminary analyses these three groupings were kept distinct, because the rural arm of the resistance has had a slightly different history and was naturally more overt. For the presentation the urban and rural resistance groups have been consolidated in order to simplify the tables. However, where important differences appear they will be noted. The Liberation Army did not engage in as frequent or as intensive terrorism as the urban groups and, hence, was probably less likely to foster lasting loyalties. Liberation Army leaders were also more easily assimilated in peacetime activity. Most of the recognized Liberation Army officials were given party positions or were in very active political roles because of their activity across North Africa. The tribesmen who formed the corps of the Liberation Army were less aware of the full implications of their activity, and, in fact, were much easier to assimilate in post-independence society.

The formation of a resistance organization across the entire northern edge of the African continent, for which the Moroccan resistance was first designed, presupposes a fairly high level of social and economic development. A comparable organization in the sub-Saharan Africa, for example, would be difficult to train and supply. Even in North Africa

---

[2] The discarded portion of the total returns (337) divides as follows according to participation in violence.

	Discarded Sample (N = 244)	Analysis Sample (N = 93)
No response	32%	9%
Liberation Army	9	14
Resistance	5	—
Both	11	28
None	43	48

activity was restricted by geography and by the general level of development of the volunteers. Ninety per cent of those engaging in violence were located in advanced provinces at the time of the questionnaire's administration. Some may have moved, but the very large difference from the non-violent suggests the importance of the regional variable. Roughly half of the non-violent were in advanced provinces. The urban-rural differentiation also supports the argument, for over a fourth of those active in the resistance were in cities, while about an eighth of the non-violent were urbanized.[3] To be in the resistance one had to be in a strategic region and where the organizational needs of planned, prolonged resistance activity could be filled. There were also certain minimal personal qualifications in order to be effective with the use of organized violence.

The organizational data comes from the Istiqlal and so must be interpreted only in terms of the party's activity. This is not too restricting a qualification since the party was eager to bring the resistance leaders into the party ranks, and made a major effort to assimilate them successfully. In 1952 and 1953 the Istiqlal was quite easily decapitated by the extremely efficient French police and military. As a result most of the resistance leaders came from lower positions in the party. One of the raging controversies among Moroccan political parties has been their respective claims as contributors to the resistance. The Istiqlal brought many resistance members into prominent party positions immediately after independence, and their training and indoctrination has been a major party problem. Their hierarchical position in 1958 gives some of the first hard evidence as to the dimensions of this problem and also to the legitimacy of the Istiqlal's claim of pre-eminence in the resistance. It appears, first, that having been engaged in violence gave one only negligible advantage in achieving higher party office. Nearly half of both groups had achieved office at the section level.[4] Even in the advanced provinces the non-participants and participants both appear to have had about a fifty-fifty chance of achieving section office, although the re-

---

[3] Of the 39 respondents in the resistance 35 were from advanced provinces; of the 46 non-participants, 24 were from retarded provinces. Chi square = .01. Of the 39 participants, 11 worked in urban settings and of the 46 non-participants, 6 were urban officials. Chi square = .001.

[4] Of the participants, 19 were section officials and of the non-participants 20 were section officials. Chi square is not significant.

sistance participants were concentrated in the advanced provinces.

The differentiating factor from the Istiqlal point of view was the re-spondent's date of recruitment, by which the resistance participant's earlier presence in the party ranks can be checked. Table VII-1 permits much more accurate interpretation of the Istiqlal's role in the resistance than has heretofore been possible. The non-violent groups is roughly equally distributed in each recruitment period except the first. A long history in the party definitely seems to have been an important factor in bringing a person into the resistance organization. Some long-time members did not participate because they were easily spotted by the police and, thus, very likely arrested before violent activities became highly organized.

Table VII-1
DATE OF RECRUITMENT AND RESISTANCE PARTICIPATION
BY PERCENTAGES

	Participant Per Cent (N=39	*Non-Participant Per Cent (N=45)*
Before 1948	64	22
1948-1954	31	38
1955 on	5	40

Chi square = .001

Possibly of more importance in understanding current affairs is the Istiqlal's poor record in bringing resistance people into the party who were *not* members of the party before the active struggle. The party may have even lost members who chose not to come back into the party's ranks. Nearly all of the post-independence recruitment has been among persons who were not in the resistance, and the party appears to have been unsuccessful in drawing resistance persons into positions of re-sponsibility. An analysis by province and recruitment does not alter the findings. In the advanced provinces an early Istiqlal joiner had about a three to one chance of being in the resistance, and a late joiner had about the same chance of not being in the resistance. The two persons recruited since 1945 who were participants in violence were Liberation Army people and not in the urban resistance group. Very possibly they may have come into prominence in a more distant region in organizing the guerrilla army and were brought into the party during an abortive attempt to recruit on a massive scale among the Army of Liberation.

91

Early recruitment and participating in the resistance did not give one any particular advantage in achieving higher office.[5] No differences occur for the early recruits, who seem to have about a fifty-fifty chance of taking higher office regardless of experience in violent organizations. The two resistance recruits since 1954 were made sub-section chiefs, while all section officials recruited in this period were from the non-participants. It seems that the Istiqlal has not made a special effort to recognize and promote members of the resistance. Even more important, it seems that the party has not been successful in getting resistance people without a pre-independence party history to take office. The findings underscore the organizational identity of the resistance in post-independence Morocco. A party would no doubt need to be much more effective in national politics than the Istiqlal has been to draw members from the highly disciplined and loyal resistance groups.

The memberships and reading habits of resistance participants gives some idea as to how their earlier experience may relate to their present pattern of interpersonal relationships. The participants were much more likely to have many memberships, which is consistent with their experience in group activity in the resistance and Liberation Army. The fact that they do have more memberships refutes the speculation that they withdraw from social activity as a result of their experience. Their high membership rates are probably one of the most important indicators of the extent to which they have been successfully assimilated into normal, peacetime living. Only five per cent of the participants gave no memberships, while over sixty per cent of the non-participants had no memberships. One half of the participants had at least one or two memberships, which might, but did not always, include their resistance organization, and over a third had three or more memberships. For the non-participants a fourth had one or two memberships and only five per cent had three or more memberships. It is noteworthy that even among the party officials having only Liberation Army experience (13 persons) there were no persons without memberships and nearly half with more than one membership.

---

[5] Of those participating in the resistance, 25 of 39 were recruited before 1948; of the non-participants, 10 o f45 were recruited before 1948. Chi square = .001. Ot the participants, 17 of 33 respondents took office by mid-1956; of the non-participants, 15 of 44 took office by mid-1956. Chi square is not significant.

Table VII-2
MEMBERSHIPS AND RESISTANCE PARTICIPATION
BY PERCENTAGES

	Participant *Per Cent (N=39)*	*Non-Participant* *Per Cent (N=46)*
None	5	61
1 or 2	56	28
3 or more	38	11

Chi square = .001

Undoubtedly one of the most important factors in the acquisition of membership is the number of groups open to the party officials. It appears that the generally poor record of the non-participants may be partially explained by the lower opportunity they have to acquire memberships. Where more groups exist for those with experience in the resistance, over three-fourths have high rates of membership. For the non-violent, on the contrary, slightly more than half have joined groups at a high rate where there are the same opportunities. The chances of the participant having more memberships are also greater where few groups have been organized. There are, of course, several factors that contribute to these findings. Even so, the findings do not provide much evidence of social maladjustment on the part of the resistance veterans, and suggest that the Istiqlal may have worked to integrate resistance participants in post-independence Morocco.

From these findings it might be anticipated that the resistance party official would also read more. An analysis of publications listed as frequently read by the two groupings does not support this conclusion, although no fully satisfactory explanation can be found. A third of the participants gave no publications, while a fifth of the non-participants did so. Slightly more than a fourth of the participants gave one or two publications, but over two-fifths of the non-participants indicated this number of regularly used publications. High rates of reading were roughly equal.[6] Since reading might be considered an indicator of general social advancement, the findings suggest that there may still be some respects in which the participants are less active. To explore this

---

[6] Of the participants, 33 per cent (13) gave no publications, 28 per cent (11) gave 1 or 2; and 38 per cent (38) gave three or more. Of the non-participants, 22 per cent (10) gave no publications; 43 per cent (20) gave 1 or 2; and 35 per cent (16) gave three or more. Chi square is not significant.

line of speculation one must turn to the demographic structure of the two groupings.

The educational background of the non-participants shows differences that help explain the curious reading habits. Most of the university educated are non-participants, and these persons very likely read more. However, the resistance appears to have drawn very heavily on secondary level persons, who are less enthusiastic readers. The resistance participant generally had more education, and over one half had some advanced education. This conforms to the expectation that a person would need certain educational skills to be an effective, reliable member of clandestine terrorist groups. From the fully detailed table it appears that the person with secondary education was more likely to join the resistance if he had gone to a party-sponsored free school than to a government secondary school.

Table VII-3

EDUCATION AND RESISTANCE PARTICIPATION BY PERCENTAGES

	Participant *Per Cent (N=31)*	*Non-Participant* *Per Cent (N=40)*
Elementary	45	70
Secondary	45	12
University	10	17
Chi square = .01		

The second aspect of Table VII-3 that may seem particularly surprising is the fact that education seems to make one less likely to have resistance experience after a certain point. Those with less education were no doubt frequently disqualified by their lack of minimal skills. But the educational factor does not work consistently in favor of resistance participation, which is especially noteworthy in view of the leading role that university educated persons, from both French and Moroccan universities, have played in the nationalist movement. The number of responses was small, and there were two university educated persons who gave no response to their resistance history. Even so, it appears that the trend was reversed at the university level. The significance of the results may be qualified by the fact that those with university education were more likely to be arrested before the resistance began as a result of their more prominent and more lengthy role in the Istiqlal. In a country where very few have advanced education, such persons are more conspicuous and more easily observed so that their usefulness to the resistance may not have been equal to that of the less easily traced village merchant.

Participation in the resistance, whether urban or rural, was a strenuous, trying experience that required the stamina of youth. Frequently it also required the daring and selfessness that are sometimes more easily mustered by younger persons. For these reasons the age findings are not too surprising in themselves, but do confirm earlier speculation on sources of tension in the Istiqlal.[7] An analysis of age and level of office revealed certain compensating factors for the relative deficiency of youth among the non-participants. Under some conditions age appears to outweigh a resistance record in achieving higher office. Thus, only about a third of the youngest resistance participants had become section officers, while half of the youngest, non-participant group had been promoted. In the middle age group the non-participants predominate in absolute and relative terms as the section level of party organization. Among the eldest there appeared to be approximately an equal chance of either the participant or non-participant becoming a section officer. In general it seems that the organizational needs of the party have enabled many non-participants to advance in the party hierarchy. There is little evidence that resistance veterans have been given promotion privileges.

Occupation seems to have been even more telling in the selection of the resistance members than education. There were factors in addition to occupational skill favoring those in modern occupations. These people tended to move about the country more freely and more frequently than those in more fixed, traditional occupations. Modern occupation was not likely to predispose a person to participate in the more remote areas, where even those in modern jobs apparently found it difficult to take up roles in the resistance. The traditionally occupied were quite clearly seriously handicapped in the resistance, although those in advanced provinces had a fifty-fifty chance of participating. In the more advanced provinces where the resistance organization was concentrated, the unoccupied officials were no more likely to be in the resistance than the traditionally occupied.

---

[7] Of the participants, 20 were 35 years of age or younger, and 18 were over 35. Of the non-participants, 20 secretaries were 35 or less, and 25 were older. Chi square is not significant.

Table VII-4
OCCUPATION AND RESISTANCE PARTICIPATION BY PERCENTAGE

	Participant Per Cent (N=37)	Non-Participant Per Cent (N=46)
Modern	46	26
Traditional	22	48
Unoccupied	32	22

Chi square = .10

An extensive exploration was made of attitude toward office among the participants and the non-participants because the party's success in assimilating the resistance veteran might be revealed in how the officials evaluate their party position. The differences in aspiration for office and confidence of preparation noted in Chapter V were not as great as might be expected. The problem bears further inquiry since the resistance people are quite possibly more accustomed to the arbitrary exercise of authority and could create problems for the Istiqlal. The prestige and authority of Istiqlal office might appeal to them more strongly than to the non-participants, and the resistance veterans also have solid grounds for feeling better prepared. One of the obstacles to probing this relationship is the fact that many of the resistance persons had previous office in the Istiqlal, so it is not possible to see how participants without previous office adjusted to party life. However, both previous office and resistance experience might be expected to affect one's attitude toward party office, and it is pertinent to examine whether or not resistance experience affects confidence and aspiration.

The differences in previous office records were large. Over three-fourths of the participants had held previous office, but less than half of the non-resistants had held office.[8] One way of exploring this finding is to see how previous office and participation relate to promotion in the party. By holding the previous office factor constant one can see that having held office favored the participant more than the non-participant at the section level, but that not having held office also hurt a resistance participant relatively more at the sub-section level. The slight relative advantage of the non-participants who did not hold previous office might be accounted for by the fact that many of them are in remote areas

---

[8] Of the participants 27 had held previous office and 12 had not; of the non-participants 21 had held office and 25 had not.

where local officers were needed more and where very few persons had resistance experience.

The party official with resistance background also appears only slightly more confident of his preparation for his present office. Roughly two-thirds of each grouping felt prepared for their present office.[9] Confidence in office is a function of many factors, including previous office, which is an indicator of experience in the party hierarchy, and level of office, which is an indicator of success in the hierarchy. Level of office is not important in the self-judgments expressed by the two groupings at the section level. If being in the resistance does affect the party hierarchy, then it seems that such handicap tends to disappear when the local official reaches the higher level of organization. The large differences occur at the sub-section level, where the participant party secretary feels well prepared in three-fourths of the cases. The resistance factor does seem to carry significance in the self-estimates expressed by sub-section officers, but once an official reaches higher office the resistance experience does not seem to be as important. The status of higher office may quite possibly compensate for the status of the resistance veteran.

An analysis of attitude toward office helps specify the party's role in assimilating resistance participants. Those who have had previous office, and therefore might be thought to have a higher self-estimate of their preparedness, are less likely to feel prepared if they have been in the resistance. Conversely, those who have not had previous office tend to feel better prepared for higher office if they were in the resistance. Put differently, the resistance participant with previous office is likely to feel less confident than the similar non-participant party official, and the resistance participant without previous office is more likely to feel confident. The full explanation of these trends is lacking, but they are consistent in that the less experienced secretary gives himself a relatively higher rating. It seems possible that the resistance may have been a kind of moderating influence in the party, rather than a disruptive influence. The resistance participants are less likely to feel confident of their qualifications, in the absence of party experience, and, therefore, may be easier to handle within the Istiqlal.

---

[9] Of the participants, 71 per cent (24 of 35 respondents) felt prepared for their present office, and of the non-participants 60 per cent (25 of 42) felt prepared. Chi square is not significant.

The evaluation of the resistance veteran's role in the Istiqlal must be made with some reservation. The most important qualification is that the sample is entirely from the Istiqlal, and it is, therefore, impossible to hold the party variable constant. The respondents have the consolation and security that party membership brings, and they also have the prestige of office. Most Istiqlal resistance members joined the party prior to the terrorist epoch, which gave ample opportunity for party loyalties to develop. The limitation is not entirely a handicap, however. The data suggest, first, that the nationalist movement may have played an important role in bringing some of the resistance participants back to constructive, peacetime vocations. The problems of the non-Istiqlal terrorist can only be interpreted by implication, but the data shed light on what the party has done, which is by no means a negligible contribution. Secondly, the available evidence helps explain what tensions, if any, were felt in the party as a result of the resistance experience.

The general adjustment of the resistance veteran was very likely helped along by the great likelihood that he was situated in an advanced province where there are more opportunities and more activity. Even so, it was seen that the violent and the non-violent had roughly an even chance at acquiring higher office in the advanced provinces. In the retarded provinces, where the party might have had difficulty because of fewer jobs and need for trained local officials, the resistance was not active. It is also in the more remote regions where the resistance veteran would find less to occupy his time and, as has become apparent since independence, would also find more local unrest which his talent for violence might effectively mobilize. Morocco has been fortunate that the resistance was generally confined to the more advanced regions, which was not the case in Tunisia and Algeria. The problem of promotion to office was also simplified and potential trouble avoided by the regional distribution. In the advanced provinces the party hierarchy was established and in many cases local officials had pre-independence claims, which tended to eliminate controversy over local prestige. In the retarded provinces where promotions were more numerous and possibly made with less planning the resistance distinction could have become important. In these regions the resistance participants were scarce, and potential rivalry thereby avoided.

There is some evidence that the resistance participant has found it reasonably easy to readjust to peacetime living. The participant attracted to the party, which may in itself help differentiate the more adjustable veteran, had more memberships than the non-participant, and displayed a generally higher rate of exploitation of opportunities to join other groups. Social adaptability notwithstanding, the Istiqlal has not always favored the resistance member. Among those with higher education and youth, the non-participants have had the relative advantage in acquiring higher office. However, in respect to experience as measured by previous office, the resistance group was more successful. These findings suggest that there was no across the board policy of favoring the resistance member in the party, and that he was treated much like any other party member.

There were several potential sources of tension. In the advanced provinces the resistance participant had previously held office more frequently than the non-participant. At the sub-section level of office the participant also tended to express more confidence in his preparation. These findings are undoubtedly closely related, but it is important for present purposes to note that there were potential grounds of discontent. When the Istiqlal split in early 1959 one of the arguments most frequently cited by the leaders of the schism was the party elders' failure to give sufficient recognition and responsibility to more active party militants. The more active militant seems very likely to have been the resistance member, and it is known that the dissident faction tried very had to have resistance leaders included in the party leadership.[10] The splinter group made a strong appeal to the resistance, and may very likely have used such grievances, real or imagined.

On the whole the participants' demographic background fits the commonly accepted image of a resistance veteran. He tended to be well educated by Moroccan standards, most often from the party operated free schools. The official who had received a university education seems to have become too conspicuous to be of much value in the resistance. The participant also tended to be young and to be from a modern oc-

---

[10] One of the leading figures in the National Union was Fqih Mohammed Basri, who was reportedly a key figure in the Casablanca terrorist organization. However, other important resistance figures refused to cooperate with the Istiqlal, notably Dr. Khatib and Ahardane, who had closer lines with the Moroccan Army of Liberation. Party rivalry over resistance claims was in part stimulated by the desire to have a voice in the distribution of benefits and privileges to resistants. There were bitter party differences over these important favors, but the quarreling was brought to an end when the Palace decided to form a Council under royalist direction.

cupational group. These are all qualifications that have obvious value in a resistance organization. They are also characteristics that might have been exploited in the party split. Several of the leaders of the new National Union are resistance figures, and they have worked to bring resistance veterans into the new party. The best evidence of their success is the fact that the Istiqlal had few local officials with resistance experience who joined the party since the fighting stopped in 1955. It is impossible to tell how many officials or members of resistance background may have left the Istiqlal, but it is clear that those who stayed were nearly all persons who had party loyalties dating from an earlier period.

VIII
Diminishing, Returns of Nationalist Unity

The Istiqlal, like many other nationalist movements in Africa and Asia, acquired its solidarity under the pressure of a colonial regime. The self-justifying and self-disciplining quality of the liberation struggle enabled the Istiqlal to expand its organization among a wide variety of people. As previous chapters have suggested, it might have been most difficult to combine the social and attitudinal differences of the movement in an effective organization in the absence of the colonial abuse, real or imagined. Not until after independence does unity become a subject for discussion, although many nationalist leaders have difficulty in conceptualizing national unity in terms that permit a variety of views and differences of opinion. The bitterness which the Istiqlal has heaped upon opponents and new political forces in Morocco testifies to the exclusiveness of the party's self-image as the guardian of national virtue and unity.

The post-independence situation generally involves many factors that continue to underscore the need for agreement. The material resources of the developing nation are most always very limited, and the immediate opportunities for their use restricted. The new nation must encompass a much wider range of social difference in political life, and do so without tried institutions. Often, it is only some vague, emotional goal like the national unity theme that can be communicated to the vast majority of new citizens. Apprehensions about national survival are often stimulated by ill-judged efforts of colonial powers to perpetuate their influence, or by even more disastrous attempts to re-conquer the lost colony. Thus, the setting is one in which leaders may be more concerned with the nation's unity than with diversification and articulation from which a new, more constructive basis for consensus might emerge.

A matrix was constructed from two preference questions involving the preservation of national unity. In the first question the respondents were asked to rank the importance of five subjects to the future of the nation, one of the choices being the restoration of Morocco's historic frontiers. As the country has encountered obstacles to rapid development and as internal politics have become more divisive there was increasing discussion of the frontiers issue. In the early months of independence the King tended to avoid the subject or to discuss it in only elliptical terms. However, Allal Al-Fassi constantly played on the issue and made it the *raison d'être* of the Istiqlal even though there were many younger party leaders who clearly thought it an unnecessary distraction. Despite the initial coldness expressed toward the issue by leaders having more specific, concrete interest, the campaign started by Al-Fassi caught on and gained wide popular approval. In time the King himself made a dramatic pilgrimage to the southern borders of Morocco and several defectors from Mauritania, which constitutes the bulk of the claimed territory, were given sinecures in the Moroccan government. By the time the questionnaire was administered there were few, if any, political leaders who would oppose the issue.[1] More than any other single issue in post-independence Morocco the recovery of her historic frontiers symbolized national unity. The irredentist question was ideally suited to such an appeal for it rests on unquestionably patriotic motives, cannot be obstructed by any of the divisions among the Moroccan people or parties, and has a grain of truth which can still be manipulated for more immediate purposes by national leaders.

The second question used in constructing the national unity matrix concerned the future of the Istiqlal. The respondent was asked to rank five subjects, one of them national unity, elaborated to include the op-

---

[1] For an account of how the issue intruded upon Moroccan internal politics, see Douglas E. Ashford, "The Irredentist Appeal in Morocco and Mauritania," *Western Political Quarterly*, v. 15, no. 4, 1962, pp. 641-651; and also I. William Zartman, "The Sahara—Bridge or Barrier," *International Conciliation*, January, 1963. When the Istiqlal reluctantly went into opposition to the King in 1963, it was to a large extent because of the King's growing conviction that he could not energetically pursue other foreign policy goals with the restrictions and conflict created by the irredentist claim.

position threat, reform of the administration, and "Moroccanization". The latter term is used to refer to the rapid replacement of French civil servants on loan to the Moroccan government, and to the use of Arabic for all official purposes. Administration reform, which is interpreted as the elimination of French influence in Moroccan bureaucracy, and Moroccanization are clearly important aspects of national unity, although expressed here in more concrete terms than in the issue of frontier recovery. All these questions have frequently been used with some opportunism and passion, especially when relations with France deteriorate or when the Moroccans wished to exert pressure on behalf of their comrades in Algeria.

The importance attached to the unity preferences was indicated by the large percentage of overlap of very high rankings when the matrix was constructed. At total of thirty-six persons indicated that both issues were of either first or second rank importance. These thirty-six persons will constitute those placing high emphasis on national unity, and the rest of the sample will be compared to them. The other groupings in the matrix were kept separate throughout the analysis. Where they manifest pculiar characteristics, especially for those representing respondents giving low rankings in both situations, the more detailed findings will be noted. However, the chapter will stress the ways in which the most extreme devotees (36 persons) to national unity differ from their colleagues (57 persons) in the party.

The possible influence of the opposition party factor on the respondent's judgments concerning national unity can be further examined by analyzing the number of opposition parties existing for each grouping. The evidence suggests that the group placing the highest value on national unity has been subjected to more opposition party activity than the group ranking the national unity choices lower. Since the high national unity group reacted similarly when assigning a role to the opposition and ranking the opposition's relative importance, and have also been subjected to more opposition activity, it appears that they are somewhat more tolerant of opposition activity than those persons giving less emphasis to national unity. The results may seem contradictory to a reader accustomed to the political values of advanced political systems. However, similar findings in Chapter IX also show that those assigning a more active role to the opposition also held fewer elections for local offices. The association of value and practice that has been ingrained into the

103

Western observer must not be arbitrarily imposed on the citizen of a developing nation.

The Moroccan party official may acquire more respect for national unity and the opposition simultaneously, although he may not be aware of the potential conflict of these views. The opposed views may be a manifestation of discontinutiy as a consequence of rapid political development. The strain may indeed exist for many new participants in non-Western political systems and may be characteristic of those undergoing rapid social advance, patterned on Western experience, while also undergoing rapid political change, which must accomodate itself to conditions in the new nation. There is need for more investigation in this area, but the respondent may be honestly expressing his appreciation and knowledge of Western political procedures, which is acquired as part of his general improvement, while also having his own sensitivity to the peculiar problems of his country, which make a constructive opposition role difficult to devise. This interpretation is highly speculative, but it will be noted below that where major differences do appear between the two groups the high national unity group is the more experienced, and very likely the more sophisticated.

One of the best pieces of evidence is the provincial and rural-urban characteristics of those placing high importance on national unity. Over three fourths of the high unity group compared to half of the low unity group were working in advanced provinces.[2] This appears to be almost a prerequisite to acquiring the high unity value, since those in retarded provinces almost all gave less emphasis to national unity. Of the twenty-nine replies from retarded provinces twenty-four placed less emphasis on national unity. The difference is much greater than that found in the study of opposition attitude, where provincial setting was of little import.

The rural-urban breakdown also revealed that the village secretary was much more likely to rank national unity of less importance, while the urban secretaries divided roughly in half. There is nearly a two to one chance that the village party official will take a much less severe view toward the national unity slogan than his urban counterpart. The three variable analysis adds a refinement of particular value in antici-

---

[2] Of the high unity group (39), 31 were from advanced provinces, and of the low unity group (57) 33 were from advanced provinces. Chi square is not significant. Of the high unity group, 9 were in urban settings, and of the low unity group, 11 were in urban settings. Chi square=.01.

pating the kind of person most susceptible to the unity appeal. He is likely to be from an advanced province, and, therefore, more likely informed about political affairs. He is also very unlikely to be from a village, and, therefore less likely to be aware of his underprivileged state compared to his more modern contemporaries.

The date of office did not appear to be of much import, but both the date of recruitment and the date of organization show interesting characteristics. Although the official ranking unity high did not generally achieve office as soon as the other grouping, the high unity official has a longer party history. Over half of the high unity group was recruited into the Istiqlal in 1947 or earlier, while about a third of the low unity group joined this early. Nearly all of the remaining high unity group joined in the 1948-1954 period, most of them before 1952.[3] There is little doubt that the early party history characterizes the high unity people, which suggests the extent to which this appeal is rooted in the early independence struggle more than the more organized, more widely experienced later phases of the nationalist movement. Nearly all the persons joining the party since 1954 (21 of 22 cases) were in the low unity group. The popular conception of the unity appeal has frequently been that it takes hold and has meaning once the nationalist organization has gained momentum. The available data suggest, to the contrary, that the issue was most persuasive among those whose experience dates from before the period of popular enthusiasm and widespread organization. A lasting devotion to national unity seems more likely to be found among those who had to create such a devotion at a very early time in their lives and when the slogan had little promise of being fulfilled.

In Chapter IX, it appears that the official with more time in the party and also more responsibility, as indicated by level of office, tended to take the more severe position vis à vis the opposition. A three variable analysis of date of recruitment, level of office and unity attitude showed that this was not entirely the case in respect to national unity. Those who have more responsibility and longer party membership divided roughly in half between the high and low unity groups. Those who

---

[3] Of the high unity group, 53 per cent (19) were recruited in the pre-1947 period, 14 per cent (16) in the 1948-1954 period, and 3 per cent (1) since 1954. Of the low unity group, 36 per cent (20) were recruited in the earliest period, 25 per cent (14) in the intermediate period, and 35 pr cent (21) in the later period. With the last two periods collapsed chi square is not significant.

joined the party later, but also enjoy section level office, tended to gravitate toward the low unity group in approximately three-fourths of the cases (18 of 25). However, it should be noted that the distribution is relatively the same for those in the sub-section office. The time factor favored taking a stronger position on national unity, but the responsibility factor did not. This is partial evidence that the national unity issue may serve an important function by enabling the generally less distinguished and possibly less secure party official to assert his party loyalty. For a variety of reasons the more successful or secure party official is less attracted to the issue of national unity than the sub-section official, especially in cases where the section official joined the party more recently. Possibly he realizes that it is not as likely to lead to constructive national action.

If the national unity theme is not spread through party channels, there must be some other communication channel providing the party secretaries with information. An analysis of the officials' reading habits suggests that the high unity group consists of two kinds of persons: those who are very isolated even in terms of their reading habits, and those who are avid readers. The general pattern of reading among the low unity respondents is very different. There is much less reading, but not much more reading at high levels. This is an interesting indication of the kind of change that seems to have taken place among the low unity respondents. They do not exceed the high unity proportionately in the extremes of advancement, but there are many more who are beginning to use media other than the ever present radio. The persons who took conflicting positions on national unity, i.e., placed it high in only one of the two contexts used in the matrix, were the persons who read the most. This conforms to the often demonstrated finding that the better informed person can more successfully articulate his values, and tends to see public issues in more detail.

The importance of the respondent's interpersonal relationships in evaluating his views on national unity were underlined by the relative inconsequence of several of the more common demographic variables in reference to the unity attitude. In this respect, the judgments on unity vary greatly from those on the future of democratic institutions, where there were important differences surrounding education, occupation, and under some circumstances age as well. In the case of education, for example, each educational category was nearly equally divided between each attitudinal group. Several attempts to demonstrate circumstances under which the educational variable became reasonably important failed. Linguistic differentiation yielded similar results. The age breakdown was also very close, never varying more than one percent between the two attitudinal groups.

The demographic variable that revealed the largest differences between the two attitudinal groups was occupation. The findings are consistent with previously presented evidence that the high unity respondent is both psychologically and materially more dependent on the party. In Table VIII - 1 the conflict between attitude toward opposition activity and national unit is once again in evidence. If the table is compared with Table IX - 3 it will be found that each occupational category has reversed its position on unity relative to its position on tolerance of opposition activity. Those in modern occupations, who tended to take a very dim view of opposition organization, are found to favor less stress on national unity by nearly two to one. The traditionally occupied were roughly evenly divided over the opposition, but are also found to put less emphasis on unity by two to one. The largest reversal is among the unoccupied, who have given evidence on several occasions of being highly dependent on the party for support. While they favored the organized opposition by nearly two to one previously, they are also found to lay stress on national unity in over half the available cases. Clearly they are the center of considerable tension.

Table VIII-1

OCCUPATION AND UNITY ATTITUDE BY PERCENTAGES

	High Unity Per Cent (N=34)	Low Unity Per Cent (N=57)
Modern	29	39
Traditional	29	40
Unoccupied	41	21

Chi square is not significant.

Although the sub-groupings are very small, the three variable analysis of occupation, age, and unity attitude provides some insight into how this outlook may vary as social change takes place in Morocco. The elder respondents having modern occupations divided evenly (5 and 5) between the two viewpoints, while the younger local officials in modern occupations favored less emphasis on national unity by three to one (16 of 21 cases). A similar trend can be found among the traditionally occupied. The findings are on the whole encouraging since those wishing to avoid the more passionate issues of Moroccan politics appear to be the productively employed, while the unoccupied represent a peculiarity of party organization in a developing nation that may very likely disappear as parties can organize more freely. Since the younger members of the more productive occupational groups are less susceptible to the appeal of national unity, one might hope for increasing moderation as social and economic progress takes place. The reservations expressed by the traditionally employed suggest that it may be a mistake to regard the more inflammatory issues in Moroccan political life as simply appeals to the less modern segment of the populace.

There has been some indication that those placing emphasis on national unity are in some respects less successful party officials and may, therefore, find the unifying theme reassuring. It is especially clear that the party officials who are more susceptible to the national unity appeal are more committed to the party in terms of time. Both the level of office and occupational composition of the high national unity group substantiate this interpretation. One would then expect that attitude towards office might also reflect insecurity or generally less accomplishment. The secretary placing little stress on national unity is indeed much less likely to have held previous office. Attaining higher office very likely means more party indoctrination and probably greater party loyalty, but it does not necessarily mean that the time spent working for the Istiqlal has been as rewarding as it might have been or as it has been for others.

There are two ways in which one might establish the extent to which the high unity group having previous office has been satisfied with their party careers. The first is to see to what extent their party work has resulted in achieving higher level offices. A three variable analysis shows that those who have held previous office and stress national unity are less likely to have achieved section level office than those having previous office and placing less stress on national unity.[4] Of the twenty-six persons holding previous office and section level positions, seventeen were less concerned with national unity. The relation between party performance and attraction to the unifying goal is reinforced by

---

[4] Of the high unity group, 73 per cent (24) held office previously, and of the low unity group, 53 per cent (27) held office previously. Chi square=.10.

the attitude of the sub-section officials who have held previous office. Of the thirty-five persons having held previous office and now at the lower level fifteen subscribed to greater national unity. There is, then, more evidence that the secretary favoring more stress on building national unity is less successful in the party organization.

His potential discontent is further substantiated by an analysis of date of recruitment, previous office and unity attitude. If the high unity respondent has generally been less successful in achieving higher office and has also worked for the party a very long time, his feeling of insecurity may very likely be heightened. The analysis shows that those holding previous office and subscribing to greater national unity have about a fifty-fifty chance of having been recruited before 1948. Those holding previous office and not subscribing to national unity have about a one to two chance of having come into the Istiqlal before 1948. In short, it seems that the official who is prepared to support more efforts toward national unity has a greater investment in time in the Istiqlal, but has not been as highly rewarded as the more recently recruited local official. Since the two groups are similar in several respects, such as age and education, that might be thought to influence their views, the findings as to success in office take on additional value.

The lack of confidence of the high unity group is also apparent in their evaluation of preparation for office. If the high unity group felt more secure in their office one might expect a greater proportion would feel prepared for their present office. The conflicting situation in which the high unity group appears to find itself is suggested by the comparison of previous office, confidence of preparation and unity attitude. Although the small sub-groupings must be interpreted with reservation, the general pattern of response is revealing. The high unity group did not feel unprepared even where it had not held previous office. They were more likely to admit being unprepared when they held previous office and less likely to feel prepared when they had held previous office. In many respects the pattern of response is very similar to that of poorly qualified local officials studied in Chapter V.

Two final clues to the state of mind of the high unity respondents are their experience in the resistance and their religious self-estimates. The high unity group differs in respect to religion, but not to the resistance. The national unity slogan was essential to the entire resistance action, and the training and experience served to reinforce devotion to one's country under all circumstances. The resistance was intended to expel the French and Spanish overlords and all traces of their influence from Morocco. Much of the discontent among resistance leaders since independence has been over the tardiness with which this has been done. Thus, nearly two-thirds of the high unity group and only slightly over a third of the low unity group had some resistance experience.[5] The respondents who expressed little interest in national unity in either framework were overwhelmingly non-violent.

There have been many indications that the party official placing stress on national unity was socially less privileged and politically less experienced. The high unity group was heavily composed of officials at the sub-section level. These officials tended to join fewer organizations, despite the same opportunity as others read very little, and their insecurity, which may not be conscious, was indicated by the fact that secretaries having an elementary education stressed unity, while those who had some secondary education or more tended to stress unity less. Similar implications are found in the occupational data. The unoccupied secretary, who has a strong predisposition toward favoring national unity, moved away from this position as he read more and apparently established more grounds for independent and informed judgment. The traditionally occupied secretary did the same thing.

There were several other indications of the more mature stature of the official who resisted the attractions of the national unity theme. If he joined the party at a later date, he tended to be older. If he had held previous office he tended to be more successful and to be a section chief. Among the high unity group those who held previous office had a smaller chance of having been promoted. Although aspirations were similar, the high unity non-aspirants were mostly at the lower organizational level, while the low unity non-aspirants were mostly section heads and, thereby, persons more likely to be successful as well as content in their party posts. The more moderate official is much less likely to be a fervent Muslim in his own eyes, which may indicate less susceptibility to appeals that have a high quotient of Arab nationalist doctrine. He is also much less likely to have participated in the resistance, and, thereby, has

---

[5] Of the high unity group, 21 of 34 respondents were in or participated in some aspects of the resistance; of the low unity group, 18 of 51 respondents had some resistance role. Chi square=.02.

110

escaped the indoctrination and discipline associated with the period of violent resistance to French rule. Conversely, the high unity respondents appear to have joined the party very early, and therefore to have more personal loyalty to Al-Fassi; or they joined very late and may accept the irredentist appeal uncritically.

Although the questionnaire did not measure extremist tendencies, the party experience and social background of the supporters of the unity theme suggest earlier findings on the psychological role of extremist notions.[6] The glory of the lost empire and determination to remove foreign vestiges no matter what the cost are clearly views endorsed by extremists in Morocco. Conversely, it is consistent with a considerable body of psychological findings that the more mature party official tended to reject the less rational goals, and often not even to associate the problems of internal governmental reform with the irredentist issue. This was probably not a conscious rejection of Al-Fassi's theme or lack of appreciation of Morocco's need to run her own government, but a reflection of a more discriminating nationalist. His views on political life are not easily coalesced in a single value. He is better informed and very likely more secure within the Istiqlal.

Better than any other aspect of the study, the unity analysis reveals the attitudinal effects of feeling individually and socially integrated into the life of the new nation. Where political development permits the kind of articulation of views indicated by those less driven by the unity requirement, there also tends to be other evidence that the party official is confident and generally optimistic. Being able to reduce the

---

[6] There is too vast a literature devoted to the perceptual effects of extremist feelings and values to attempt a summary here. However, we have been generally negligent in relating this literature, particularly some of more recent work on cognitive disonance, to the problems of political development in Africa and Asia. Continued dependence on emotionally forceful themes may even have a detrimental effect on other efforts to reconstruct the new nation. An extremely suggestive study which would bear repetition in a developing country is Charles D. Farris' "Selected Attitudes on Foreign Affairs as Correlates of Authoritarianism and Political Anomie," *Journal of Politics*, v. 22, no. 1, 1960, pp. 50-67. The possible disruptive effects are suggested by Paul Sheatsley, "Expectations of War and Depression," *Public Opinion Quarterly*, v. 13, Winter 1959-60, p. 83, where he tells how political anomie may be created by powerful events, producing feelings of "powerlessness, cynicism, futility, and apathy in relation to the political system." Certainly these feelings are much more prevalent in the developing country than the United States, though our psychological understanding of them in relation to political development is still rudimentary.

more amorphous unity theme to more concrete problems, which were given higher precedence, is an important component of political maturity. The threat of "neo-colonialism" and dreams of lost empire still intrude on the political life of many developing countries, and in somewhat different form are not absent from the political life of many advanced nations. It is encouraging to see that the rigidities created by heavy reliance on national unity themes, and reinforced by long years of the liberation struggle, can be minimized as the new nation turns to tasks requiring a more adaptive, less suspicious mentality.

IX

Opposition Threat — Real or Imagined?

There are a wide variety of attitudinal and sociological conditions that contribute to what Professor Lipset has called the "necessary ambiguity of democratic politics."[1] Without this elusive quality of Western political life it would probably be very difficult for the voter, and even less active political participants, to withstand the strains of parties replacing each other in office. Indeed, there are relatively few democracies where parties have rotated in office without some deep social differences or irreconcilable views occasionally threatening to disrupt political life. The American voter has, on the whole, been particularly successful in reducing the intensity of feelings about national politics, and finding various ways to express extreme views at many levels within the national political system.[2] Without this valuable confusion, or perhaps more accurately, dispersal of political views, the institutional dichotomy of our party system might well produce endless conflict rather than agreement.

The new nation of Africa and Asia finds itself in a setting where the slow process of socially diffusing the disruptive forces of political life is difficult. Nationalist movements have been nutured on intolerance

---

[1] *Political Man*, New York, Doubleday, 1960, p. 276.

[2] The clearest analysis of the voter's dispersal of extremist feelings in our political process is the discussion of ideological content in the perception of the voting process in Angus Campbell, *et. al.*, *The American Voter*, New York, Wiley, 1960, pp. 216-265. For further suggestive comment on this problem see Bernard Berelson, "Democratic Theory and Public Opinion," *Public Opinion Quarterly*, v. 16, 1952, pp. 313-330.

of opposition, and strongly hostile attitudes toward any form of opposition may well influence views on the desirability of the one party state. If this is the course that Africa and Asia will follow, then it will be many generations before Western countries will have a meaningful message for the developing country. However, these views are sometimes advanced without a careful examination of the function of political tolerance in the more developed, better integrated society, and fail to allow for the many benefits accruing to a people who find many ways to express social tensions and opposing views. This chapter is an exploration of the early development of views toward the opposition in Morocco. While the discontinuities of the politically less experienced party militant can be seen, it is also possible to locate the politically tolerant and draw some general conclusions on how political opposition is perceived in the developing country.

Moroccan opposition party activity is more widespread than might be expected. Nearly half the secretaries from the entire sample reported one political party organized locally in addition to the Istiqlal, and nearly a third reported two or more parties at work.[3] Thus, the overall level of party activity in Morocco is higher than might be assumed, although in many instances the local opposition party consisted of only one or two militants. It should also be noted that the government generally took a tolerant position toward the opposition in the period that the questionnaire was administered. Basic legal rights did not exist for parties until late 1958, and the charter granted at that time gave the Ministry of the Interior sweeping powers in emergency situations. Nevertheless, King Mohammed V took pains to acknowledge all the organized parties in the country and all were allowed to express their views freely in the press, both in Arabic and French.

---

[3] Opposition party activity was one of the most evenly distributed and most widely reported phenomenon measured by the survey. The small sample (93) being used for this study compares very closely with the large sample.

	Analysis Sample (N=93)	Discarded Sample (N=244)
No response	5%	10%
No opposition	16	9
One party	41	46
Two parties	26	20
Three or more	11	5

At the time the survey was performed, the historic feud between the Istiqlal and the P.D.I. (*Parti Démocratique de l'Indépendence*) continued and two new parties had appeared. The Popular Movement was a rurally based party with leaders who rejected the Istiqlal's readiness to accept independence prior to Algerian liberation. Nevertheless, the Popular Movement was completely loyal to the monarchy, and joined in the royalist front formed in the 1963 elections. The U.N.F.P. (*Union National des Forces Populaires*) was a splinter group from the Istiqlal, which formed an urban, worker oriented party in early 1959. Morocco is, therefore, a particularly useful example of a multiplicity of parties, and there has been ample opportunity for both historic nationalists and more recently recruited party members to become familiar with opposition party activity.[4]

The Istiqlal was concerned about opposition activity in 1958 and there were long discussions about opposition parties in Istiqlal publications. The direct choice was made quite clear: allow the opposition to do nothing to affect nationalist unity; allow it to criticize with care, but have no popular support; allow it to criticize freely and have a small organization; or allow it to organize a large opposition party. About half the respondents (39) selected the most severe policy, twenty-five chose the least active role, eight the restricted opposition party role and seven the fully operative opposition. The direct response excludes the no response group (14), who probably are the less informed and generally evasive respondents. The forty persons giving the opposition some meaningful role in the political system will be grouped together as the "tolerant" in the following analysis, but any major differences among the groups taking more permissive stands will be noted.

In addition to assigning a role to the opposition directly, the competing parties were discussed indirectly in three other questions. The secretaries were asked to rank the importance of the opposition as a problem for the party nationally, for the party locally, and as an immediate source of local party difficulties. The overall differences in the perception of the opposition suggest an important discontinuity in the party officials'

---

[4] For more detailed discussion of the organization, program and tactics of the opposition parties in Morocco see *Political Change in Morocco*, Princeton, Princeton University Press, 1959, by the author, pp. 302-343. During 1963 party politics became extremely acrimonious in Morocco, and both the Istiqlal and the U.N.F.P. found themselves opposing the new King.

views. When the opposition was judged in the framework of the Istiqlal's role nationally or locally it was placed second. (The most important national problem was economic improvement, and the most important local problem was recruiting members.) However, the militant's ranking of the oppostion in the more concrete context of his immediate difficulties placed the opposition at the bottom of the scale. (First importance was given to lack of funds.) This does not mean that strong feelings might not be generated locally by the opposition, but does suggest that the image of the opposition as a real problem rapidly dwindles in the local setting.

Although comparable data are not available, our experience with political systems having an institutionalized opposition suggests that the attitude toward opposition would be expressed conversely. The Istiqlal militant minimizes the opposition as an immediate, concrete obstacle, but most local party organizations in advanced systems probably consider the opposition as their most important immediate problem. Their thinking about other problems is highly influenced by the successes, failures, and plans of the opposition. It is on the national level and in relation to more abstract questions that the advanced party system begins to soft pedal the opposition's importance. No one is eager to see the opposition take over the national government, but one does not seem to dread it like the Moroccan nationalist official apparently does. Even on the local level opposition parties are not thought of as much in terms of what they propose to do to the country as what they may do in the way of cutting off other parties' patronage and local influence. The Moroccan nationalist thinks nationally, which is understandable given his experience in the struggle for independence. If a more moderate image of the opposition is desired and if a workable party system is to emerge, it may be desirable that the local official, and possibly many other participants, see the opposition as less of a threat on the national level, and as a meaningful target for local party exchanges.

A more precise idea of the discontinuity of each group's evaluations can be obtained from Table IX - 1. Both the tolerant and the less tolerant consider the opposition of importance when considering the party's future locally. The high and low preferences do not permit us to say that the opposition is perceived with similar degrees of conviction or intensity, but only of similar relative importance in the given list of choices in the preference question. The divergence in the two group's evaluations appears when these findings are compared with the importance attached to the opposition in the national framework. In this context the tolerant tend to downgrade the opposition, which is reasonable in view of the opposition's role in 1958 and the Istiqlal's national stature prior to the split. Thus, in the remote framework of national action the less tolerant are more severe. However, when the opposition's importance is evaluated in relation to a series of practical obstacles to local party development the less tolerant continue to stress the opposition, while the more tolerant downgrade the opposition a source of local difficulty for the Istiqlal. In neither case does the feeling toward the opposition present a continuous gradient, while the less tolerant appear either to fail to discriminate or react very sharply.

Table IX-1
IMPORTANCE GIVEN THE OPPOSITION IN THREE
FRAMEWORKS OF EVALUATION (ACTUAL FIGURES)

Tolerant	Party's Future Nationally	Party's Future Locally	Obstacle to Local Operation
High	12	27	14
Low	28	13	26
Less Tolerant			
High	17	32	18
Low	22	7	21

In evaluating the two major groups being used it may be useful to examine their actual contact and experience with opposition parties, and other activities where opposing interests might be manifested. One such situation is the periodic election of officers for local party positions. The data show that such elections have seldom been held as often as claimed by higher party officials or as required by party statutes. Some of the conflict the question created may be reflected in the rather high no response rate from the less tolerant. The local officials' first experience with democratic formalities is within the party. Over half the less tolerant have experienced two or more elections, while only a third of the more tolerant have had comparable exposure to party elections.[5] The more tolerant official appears to have received even less electoral tutoring than his less tolerant colleague. The expectation that essentially

---

[5] Of the less tolerant, 57 per cent (16 of 28 responses) had held two or more elections. It should be remembered that the division between two and three elections is arbitrary, but thought to be reasonable considering the time involved. Chi square is not significant.

117

transferable experience in more democratic features of political exchange will be transfered to the national realm seems ill-founded. Either the less tolerant fails to project the meaning of elections, which later data on his preparation suggest might occur, or he simply attaches less importance to the opposition in any national context. His heightened feelings toward the opposition compared to the tolerant group have already been portrayed in Table IX - 1.

The significance of the failure to extend the role of democratic experience may be altered, first, by the amount of time the local office of the party has been in existence. An office under a more tolerant official and organized prior to 1956 had more elections, but nearly all offices under the more tolerant and organized since then have had very few elections. If the press of events since 1956 accounted for fewer elections the less tolerant would have shown a similar decline in holding them, which he did not. The disparity is even more striking since both groups are operating in roughly the same environment of opposition parties. About a fourth of each group has no opposition, a fourth one opposition party, and about a third reported two or more opposition party groups.[6] There seems to be another important dimension in the formation of attitudes toward the opposition. The party officials were greatly influenced by the time in which they became involved in party organizational activities; the more recently involved apparently taking a less tolerant view toward the opposition than the more experienced official.

Only among those secretaries recruited into the Istiqlal before 1948 did the tolerant substantially outnumber the less tolerant. The more recently arrived party official may have acquired his view of opposition activity under the embittering regime of the later years of the Protectorate. In the late 40's and early 50's the Istiqlal was necessarily indoctrinating new militants to take firm stands against any activity weakening the party, and there was naturally less need for democratic justifications for party leadership under the oppression of the more brutal Resident Generals. The more experienced party official, however, had a much greater opportunity to acquire his views prior to the actual struggle for independence, and at a time when there was still some hope of

---

[6] Among the less tolerant, 8 officials reported no opposition; 16, one party; and 12, two or more opposition parties. Among the more tolerant, 10 reported no opposition, 13 reported one party; and 15 reported two or more parties. Chi square is not significant.

reconciliation with France. Brought up on a purer diet of French political ideas than more recent arrivals, the early recruits show more consistency in applying their notions about the opposition. The fact that so many later recruits have only paid lip service to the practices for which the liberation struggle was pursued indicates how severe the individual strain may be at the local level in many developing countries.

Half the more tolerant group were among the Istiqlal's first local officials. They were in fact well established Moroccans with European-type educations. The less tolerant attitudes began in a period of greater struggle and more rapid party expansion. Nearly half the less tolerant were enrolled during the period of more intense recruitment and training. As the data indicate, the views of the less tolerant do not alter according to the number of opposition parties present if they were later recruits. However, among those recruited earlier the presence of more parties is associated with greater acceptance of party competition. As in the case of elections within the party, the more experienced party official displays a greater tendency to relate his political experience outside the party to his life in the party. In this respect, one might say that his attitude toward the opposition is both more coherent in terms of his experience and subject to less extreme variations.

Table IX-2
DATE OF RECRUITMENT AND OPPOSITION ATTITUDE
BY PERCENTAGES

	Less Tolerant Per Cent (N=39)	More Tolerant Per Cent (N=39)
To 1948	36	51
1948-1954	44	23
1955 on	20	26

Chi square is not significant.

Consistent with their late recruitment, and at a time when educational opportunities for known nationalists were being curtailed by the French, the less tolerant have less education.[7] Those having secondary education fall approximately evenly between the two groups, and the university educated is over two-thirds more tolerant. However, education is a poor guide to practical matters in a developing country, and the university

---

[7] Of the less tolerant, 57 per cent (20) had elementary education; 34 per cent (12), secondary; 9 per cent (8), university education. Chi square is not significant.

group is vastly over-represented even for a relatively privileged country like Morocco. Education brings so many privileges and so much security to the fortunate few in a new nation, that it is not suited to identifying the conditions contributing most to the spread of tolerant values.

The occupational differentiation is possibly more useful in exploring the social attributes of the two groups. The occupational categories that are likely to expand rapidly as the country develops, e.g., merchants, officials, and teachers, were likely to be less tolerant, especially the merchants, who generally come from less privileged social backgrounds and are nearly all less tolerant. This is not the case for the minor official, who divides roughly evenly between a more and less tolerant outlook. The traditionally occupied do not appear to be affected by occupation to any marked degree, but the less understood unoccupied persons display a high degree of leniency. Indeed, they are the largest single occupational group in the more tolerant group. Of the fifteen persons granting the opposition the fully active roles, eight were unoccupied.

The traditionally occupied and poorly educated are less tolerant by nearly two to one, the highest incidence of severity toward the opposition. The less educated person who acquires modern occupational status is also very likely less tolerant, although secondary education has less effect. The university educated official having a modern occupation is tolerant in nearly all available cases. This substantiates the early finding concerning the beneficial effects of modern education, an observation that also gets indirect support from intolerant opposition attitudes expressed by the two university educated respondents who were in traditional jobs. The unoccupied secretary, who was noted in Chapter II to be very active politically, seems to have overcome his elementary education in a way that those in traditional pursuits have not. The unoccupied secretary is more tolerant by nearly a two to one ratio, and education seems to be of less significance. His confidence and party experience appears to have contributed to the formation of a tolerant view despite his educational handicap.

In the advanced provinces those in modern occupations split evenly between the two groups. But the traditionally occupied tend to magnify their intolerant tendencies in advanced provinces, where about three-fourths of them were less tolerant (10 of 13 cases). The additional party indoctrination and closer contact with modern political affairs that takes place in the advanced provinces may heighten the traditionally occupied person's apprehensions over opposition activity. He may also become increasingly aware of his socially and personally insecure position, and begin to compensate by becoming a more militant Istiqlal member. This possibility receives some indirect support by the attitudinal position of the unoccupied, of whom two-thirds are more tolerant in advanced provinces (14 or 21 cases), regardless of their less privileged backgrounds. The unoccupied share many of the characteristics of the traditionally occupied, but they do not fear the opposition nearly as much. The prestige and confidence of their party position apparently serves to reassure the unoccupied officials.

Those in modern occupations were the only occupational grouping to react favorably as the number of opposition parties increased. This is consistent with the more confident, more sophisticated thinking that one might expect from higher occupational achievement. The growth of opposition does not as easily lead them into taking an extremely hard line. In comparison the traditionally occupied seem to take a dim view of the opposition regardless of the number of parties, while the unoccupied demonstrate that their tolerant tendencies are much more likely to be expressed by those having fewer opposition parties to deal with. When higher levels of opposition party organization are reached, the unoccupied party official, who may depend on the Istiqlal for his support or possibly owe some sinecure to the party, tends to be undecided in his opposition outlook.

The chances of the less tolerant diffusing their attitudes toward the opposition through party contacts do not seem very great. The less tolerant are, first, more heavily concentrated in the middle age bracket, whereas the tolerant tend to be older and in less influential positions. The less tolerant assert their presence in several ways. They are likely to have higher aspirations, and to have held office previous to their present duties.[8] They have had roughly a fifty-fifty chance of reaching office at the section level, while the tolerant have done less well. Although it is

---

[8] Of the less tolerant, 56 per cent (19) felt prepared for present office and the rest did not. Of the more tolerant, 69 per cent (24) felt prepared. Chi square is not significant. Of the less tolerant, 68 per cent (25) held previous office. Of the more tolerant 56 per cent (19) held previous office. Chi square is not significant. In reviewing the experience of the two groups and how it relates to their present attitudes, it is also significant that the tolerant had much less exposure to the resistance. Of the tolerant, 36 per cent (13) had participated in the resistance; of the less tolerant, 58 per cent (21) had resistance experience.

not possible to tell whether modesty, lack of confidence or other interests restrains the tolerant party official, he feels as well prepared for office as the less tolerant and his record of attaining office previously is nearly the same. The fact that the tolerant does not assert his position as firmly within the party as the less tolerant, despite comparable experience and preparation, suggests the behavior of a person less dependent on the expression of extremist views, and probably less determined to press his own values within the party.

Our knowledge of the development of democratic values and other more complex attitudes in developing nations is still rudimentary, but it can be vastly improved by adapting survey techniques to conditions existing in new nations. The way in which the Istiqlal officials express tolerance of opposition activity may suggest some lines of further inquiry although more data are needed to establish more reliable conclusions. The more impressive aspect of the Istiqlal data is the consistent image of the kinds of persons taking more or less tolerant views.

The less tolerant persons tend to hold more elections for their members, but they do not appear to reconcile tolerance within the party with tolerance of opposition parties. The less tolerant appears to have a kind of double standard enabling him to reconcile his use of political competition within the party with the denial of competitive politics outside the party. His behavior suggests the conformitive, ritualized observance of democratic practices, which reduces feelings of conflict when such practices are denied to those outside his organization.[9] He was often recruited in the period of the Istiqlal's growth demanding special discipline, and has generally achieved higher office. He was usually traditionally occupied or had less education if he had a modern education. The less tolerant has high aspirations for future office but a comparatively low estimate of his preparation, although he has also tended to hold more previous office. The less tolerant is the more experienced, more disciplined official, but he also appears to be the secretary whose

---

[9] In this connection it should be noted that in the more diversified political system such as one finds in Morocco there may be political forces impinging on less tolerant attitudes. Thus, the Istiqlal's experience of being placed in the opposition on several occasions since 1960 has made its leaders much more aware of civic rights and the privilege of office. They were unresponsive when smaller parties made similar complaints in 1957 and 1958, when the Istiqlal had the force of government on its side. The fact that parties do change office in Morocco may have an impact on the less tolerant views encouraged when the party enjoyed power.

social status and political orientation has been uncritically absorbed from Istiqlal.

The more tolerant person may also have party experience, but of a different kind. He tended to join the party at an early date, and, therefore, more likely formed his own political views and underwent a measure of political maturation before becoming enveloped in party affairs. The more highly educated were very likely to be more tolerant, as are the unoccupied who have a long party history. The most notable characteristic of the more tolerant was the extent to which his tolerance was consistently expressed, even in non-party matters. Where he also has higher aspiration, he expressed more confidence in office and was better prepared in fact. He expressed his tolerance of the opposition in the presence of opposition parties, and he also tended to hold elections for local office regardless of the disrupting effect of local opposition activity. It would be unfair and contradictory to the purpose of this investigation to assert that the less tolerant party secretary was hypocritical, since he may see no contradiction between his views on the opposition and his other activity. But it is meaningful and correct to state that the more tolerant comes much closer to expressing the attitudinal consistency associated with a more tolerant individual in our own society.

The findings suggest possibilties for more precise and more comprehensive research into the attitudinal structure of persons undergoing rapid change. The Istiqlal official was unusually dependent on the party for his views of the external world as well as Moroccan politics. The structural quality of opinion formation during periods of extreme nationalism is very likely much like that observed in Israel by Professor Eisenstadt and his colleagues: the ritualistic adoption of new norms correlated with persons having an "almost unitary reference group."[10] There is little doubt but that the Istiqlal has been nearly the sole organized group in the formation of new attitudes among the Istiqlal militants. The nationalist struggle was not the kind of action that permitted the participant to adopt the differentiated attitudes of the person who partici-

---

[10] "Reference Group Behavior and Social Integration: An Explorative Study," *American Sociological Review*, v. 19, no. 2, 1954, pp. 180-181. For a further elaboration also useful in interpreting the Istiqlal militants' experience, see Eisenstadt, "Studies in Reference Group Behavior: I Reference Norms and the Social Structure," *Human Relations*, v. 7, no. 2, 1954, pp. 191-216.

pates in many groups and sees many opportunities to acquire status. Indeed, it is possible that those officials recruited prior to the period of severe conflict and educated in the much less rigorous setting of the early period of the nationalist movement find it easier to minimize the attitudinal "risk" of involvement in a modern society than the more recent recruits. As we are able to specify more accurately the discontinuities of experience and new national values in the development of Africa and Asia we shall be better prepared to relieve the conflict such tensions create and to encourage the formation of political systems that are at once more adaptive and more democratic.

X

The Social Roots of Consensus

One of the key assumptions in earlier inquiries into the political process of developed nations has been the existence of consensus. The fact that most European nations managed to reach agreement on most national problems has given a misleading singularity to our interpretation of consensus. Not until the attitudinal probing connected with the study of American voting behavior did we develop a more precise notion of consensus, which may have application to the formation of consensus in developing countries. Thus, a recent study of nation-building acknowleges that "the building of consensus does not call for a single, common orientation of all toward the state and toward the political realm."[1] There are now findings and methods, as well as a growing body of psychological theory, which suggest that the simplified concept of consensus is neither fruitful nor accurate. The present chapter is an exploration of some of the complexities of consensus formation.

In raising questions about the structure of attitudes in developing countries, this chapter takes the analysis of the Istiqlal officials' views to another degree of abstraction than that represented by the comparison of attitudes and social difference directly.[2] The alternative seems par-

---

[1] Lucian Pye, (ed.), *Communications and Political Development*, Princeton, Princeton University Press, 1963, p. 124. See also his discussion of concensus in "The Non-Western Political Process," *Journal of Politics*, v. 20, No. 3, August 1958, pp. 468-486.

[2] Those interested in the amalgamation of psychological theory that is particularly appropriate to the problem raised in this chapter might wish to read M. Brewster Smith, "Opinions, Personality and Political Behavior," *American Political Science*

ticularly attractive for inquiry into attitudinal change in developing societies. On the one hand, single variable explanations based on social differences or widely supported values appear to be even less promising for the investigation of the psychological processes of change in the less developed countries than they have been in more advanced nations.[3] Although the findings presented here do not constitute a fully satisfactory explananation of the operating of consensus, they do provide a "diagnostic" analysis that may suggest further research.[4]

The purpose of this chapter is to shed some light on how consensus develops in a newly established country. In the more highly developed political systems consensus is often thought of as a commonly understood area of agreement. Within this reasonably well defined area there may be many possible courses of action, and the political system operates to select courses of action in full confidence that within the permitted area all solutions will prove acceptable to the populace. The area of agreement, within which discussion and disagreement may take place without placing severe strain on the political system, is generally taken as a given factor in the study of the more advanced political systems. In the less advanced political systems, however, it has often been noted that this important ingredient of a viable political system is lacking or present in only rudimentary form.

Since we are dealing with such a widely observable characteristic of national political systems it would be surprising if the results were too different than those that might be anticipated in studying a more highly

---

Review, v. 52, no. 1, March 1958, pp. 1-17; or the study Smith made with Jerome S. Bruner and Robert W. White, *Opinions and Personality,* New York, Wiley, 1956, especially chapter II. Additional pioneer work has been done by Irving Sarnoff, Daniel Katz, and Milton J. Rosenberg.

[3] The controversy in political science has centered on the importance of sociological and psychological investigation in the study of voting behavior, and is clearly spelled out in the recent study of Angus Campbell, et al., *The American Voter,* New York, Wiley, 1960. The evaluation of the importance of specific demographic variables in given problems has been going on in sociology for some time. See for example, John M. Foskett, "Social Structure and Social Participation," *American Sociological Review,* v. 20, 1955, pp. 431-438.

[4] A "diagnostic" survey has been defined as concerned with a number of variables whose relation to the central problem of the study, i.e., how the local leaders formulate their political attitudes, is not fully understood. For some extremely useful remarks on the various kinds of survey inquiry see Herbert Hyman's *Survey Design and Analysis,* Glencoe, Free Press, 1957, pp. 66-83.

developed system.[5] One would expect that the attitudinal structures contributing to the operation of a political system would be similar in all modern nation-states, if only because all states tend to claim roughly comparable rights, provide similar services, and make similar impositions on citizens. In general, it may be said that the local Moroccan officials seem to express agreement and disagreement about their political system in a pattern that might also be found in the more developed system. The pattern also conforms to established knowledge of how persons orient themselves psychologically in systems of action less intricate than the modern states.

One aspect of the operation of consensus in Moroccan politics has been singled out. Given a variety of alternative actions pertaining to national policy it was speculated that the non-Western respondent would give evidence of increasing disagreement as the frame of reference became more meaningful. One of the reasons consensus contributes to agreement and effective decision-making at the national level is that individual differences of view are not as meaningful at a level relatively remote from most citizens' realm of experience. The preference questions posed the same or similar selection of choices regarding national affairs in reference to the national interest, the government or a political party, for example. In each case the frame of reference is closer to the respondent's experience, easier to relate to his knowledge, and more likely to stimulate partisan interests. One would expect, then, that disagreement would increase as the frame of reference for alternative selection became more intimate.

The method of measuring consensus is based on a statistical device, the coefficient of concordance,[6] which measures the extent of similarity among a series of rank orders. The preferences are easily put into rank order for any number of respondents.[7] The procedure was to divide the

---

[5] It is encouraging to note that an inquiry along the same lines, but using Americans and a different measurement technique, has arrived at similar conclusions. See James M. Protho and Charles M. Grigg, "Fundamental Principles of Democracy: Bases of Agreement and Disagreement", *Journal of Politics*, v. 22, 1960, pp. 276-295.

[6] The procedure for calculating the coefficient of concordance and its significance has been taken from M. J. Monroney, *Facts from Figures*, Harmondsworth, England, Penguin Books, 1951, pp. 336-341. The author is indebted to Karl Schuessler and Melvin De Fleur of the Indiana University Sociology Department for advice on the coefficient's application.

[7] A standard system was used to arrive at the rank order of the choices of each

small sample along various lines of differentiation, and then to compare the rankings or preferences given by the groups formed by each differentiation. The procedure may be clearer on examining Table X-1. The horizontal axis represents seven differentiations of the small sample. The grounds for differentiation are, of course, arbitrary and limited by the information available. However, most of them are the major demographical variables regularly used in research of this kind. The important point is that each represents another way of dividing the respondents into sub-groups, and, thereby, another way of comparing the rankings or preferences. The vertical axis gives the seven frameworks in which the preferences were posed. For example, ninety one persons gave their occupation and were divided into three sub-groups, already compared in descriptive form in Chapter II. A summation of preferences was made for each of the sub-groups in each of the frameworks. The coefficient provides a single figure giving the extent to which the rankings were in the same order in each of the frameworks.

For present purposes it should be noted that the preferences involved the major national questions of the day, although the choices were modified slightly to make sense in the various frames of reference. The size of the sample as well as the respondents' party association means that it is not possible to make statistically valid generalizations from the data. The coefficient of concordance is being used simply as a synoptic device, although it is expected that similar patterns of consensus formation would be found in observing other Moroccans and other non-Western countries. A coefficient of 1.0 represents complete agreement, i.e., that all the groupings gave the same rank order preferences to the alternatives in the given framework, and decreases to zero, which represents complete disagreement. The coefficients were not accepted without regard for their internal significance, however, and all the given coefficients except the three italicized cases have a level of significance of .05 or better.

In addition to providing some thought-provoking clues as to how consensus might be constructed and observed in the developing nation,

---

preference question. A percentage score was calculated by adding up the ranking for each selection. A first ranking was given 4 points, a second ranking 3 points, etc., down to 0 for a fifth place ranking. This sum was divided by the number of respondents times the maximum rank score for 4. Thus, a selection that was ranked first by all the respondents would have an arithmetic score of 1.0.

the findings in Table X-1 confirm the basic hypothesis. As the frame of reference moves closer to the respondents' own realm of experience, they tend to express more disagreement. This is true according to the seven differentiations used here, although it must be remembered that the differentiations are selected on the basis of available data and general knowledge of how people reveal consensus in many political systems. When the choices refer to such distant frameworks as future national unity the coefficient reaches .890, and it drops precipitously to .617 when the same choices are posed in reference to the local members.

The way in which consensus is portrayed and the meaning attached to "agreement" in Table X-1 may be clearer by reflecting a moment on the meaning of the coefficient itself. For the study the area of agreement is represented by the alternative of choices themselves. In the questions dealing with the nation the respondents tend to give the same rank order to the alternatives or choices regardless of the way in which the officials had been differentiated. Thus, it might be very easy to make a decision concerning national affairs so long as the frame of discourse can be kept at this very general level. It may also be easier to resolve some difficult problems and make some hard decisions by forcing resolution to take place at this level of discourse. In a very literal sense the figures representing high degrees of agreement across the top two lines of Table X-1 may represent a kind of political behavior that is precisely what the leaders of new nations wish to elicit when they use extreme nationalist appeals. For some limited purposes it may represent the psychological process of consensus construction. There are no overwhelming reasons why this should not be done as a new nation seeks to create national political awareness and solidarity, but there may be certain problems if agreement is elicited by stressing the remote framework over long periods of time.[8]

---

[8] There is an extremely delicate and little understood balance to be achieved in the developing nation in using highly affective appeals as a stimulus for participation and attitudinal change. In so far as such appeals contribute to better social adjustment and evaluation of national problems, attitudinal change will probably assist the process of societal and political development. However, it is also possible that continued reliance on extremism will form psychological rigidities and emotional tensions. The outbursts against racial minorities in some developing countries may be encouraged by such appeals becoming simply vehicles for the externalization of unrelated fears and apprehensions. For a study of the constructive use of such appeals, see Judith T. Shuval, "The Role of Ideology as a Predisposing Frame of Reference for Immigrants,"*Human Relations*, v. 12, no. 1, 1959, pp. 51-63.

Table X-1

SOCIAL DIFFERENCES AND ISSUE EVALUATION

Differentiation of Groupings

Framework of Issue Evaluation:	Occupation N=91(3)	Language N=91(4)	Aspiration to Higher Office N=77(4)	Education N=92(4)	Participation in Violence N=93(5)	Estimate of Preparation N=93(5)	Role for Opposition N=93(5)	Mean
Unity future:	.956	.865	.928	.940	.963	.726	.856	.890
Unity past:	.956	.950	.850	.930	.913	.856	.736	.884
Govt. future:	.806	.803	.766	.759	.659	.578	.808	.739
Govt. past:	.816	.790	.828	.663	.803	.630	.616	.735
Party local:	.794	.738	.813	.825	.734	.602	.640	.735
Party members:	.778	.775	.763	.747	.547	.790	.584	.712
Party national:	.800	.750	.553	.596	.650	.574	.394	.617
Mean:	.844	.810	.785	.780	.753	.679	.662	.759

*N represents the number of respondents used in the particular grouping and the figure in parenthesis is the number of groups differentiated.

First, the operation of the modern state requires making many decisions, and it is difficult to relate every desired choice to this remote framework. Second, the social and economic progress which the new nations uniformly desire is constantly working to produce new areas within which decisions must be made or, more exactly, creating new frameworks for judgment such as those represented by the government and the party. One cannot be sure but what the nearer framework will be more persuasive, and there is some *prima-facie* evidence for thinking this may be the case. Third, the general progress of the new nation also means that new bases of differentiation are constantly created in the manner of the advanced, industrial society. In cases where the desired choice has prevailed, agreement may be shattered as social change introduces new differentiations that break up the pattern of agreement. For example, confidence in preparation for office introduces a basis of potential disagreement into thinking about the government past and future. There are, of course, many other reasons making constant, high agreement difficult, such as the simple question of how to drain off the generally more intense feelings that are aroused in creating a high degree of agreement.

There are real doubts as to whether the kind of uniform action related to more remote attitudinal frameworks is appropriate to an advanced political system.[9] The kind of agreement that seems better suited to the social and political needs of the advanced nations is one in which differences are expressed and one that enables the citizens to resolve these differences in a concrete framework. Thus, the government, the political party, and probably local groups and associations as well are all foci of our thinking about national politics. Structurally they are closer to the citizen's field of observation and easier for him to associate with courses of action responding to his particular needs and expectations. This also seems to be the case in the less developed country. There is much less

---

[9] It should perhaps be noted that nationalist values are used in all kinds of political systems, and the suggestions made here are not intended to imply that the Arab countries have been more negligent or less successful than other countries. We can observe the extreme nationalist application of such values in Western "jingoism" and the social and psychological effects of jingoism are very much like what one might observe in less developed countries. Those interested in the kind of attitudinal discontinuity contributing to such opinions might read P. L. Kendall, "The Ambivalent Character of Nationalism Among Egyptian Professionals," *Public Opinion Quarterly*, v. 20, 1956, pp. 277-292.

agreement among the party secretaries, for example, when the preferences are expressed in relation to the members' needs or the party's role. In the new nation as well as the older nation these frameworks for political and social activity are psychologically more meaningful to the citizen. He can attach his differences to these less remote frames of reference, and he can seek actual solutions insofar as these frames of reference are accessible and effective within the society.

The horizontal axis of Table X-1 raises some interesting questions when compared with political behavior in more advanced political systems. For example, occupation does not seem to be the basis of many differences of opinion, although it has often been regarded as an important factor in forming the views of Western citizens.[10] There are several possible explanations. First, it must be remembered that this is a sample of active party members, most of whom are connected with rural Morocco. Even those in modern occupations are frequently located in the countryside, and do not compare with the higher occupational groups in modern nations. As party militants all the respondents have been subjected to a considerable amount of party indoctrination that minimizes material differences, although it may not minimize other differences such as education. Education is more closely related to prestige and influence in Morocco. Psychologically speaking, the differen between advanced and elementary education in a new nation is very likely much greater than that between a Koranic teacher and a rural merchant. Thus, the horizontal axis begins to tell us something about the importance of the major demographic variables in opinion formation in a new country. Although these variables must be interpreted in reference to the social system involved, the findings provide some insights for further behavioral studies of how political views are manifested in a developing country.

Some of the actual differences of opinion that appear in the various groupings confirm interpretations suggested in previous chapters. The group of unoccupied party secretaries, for example, express certain

---

[10] This contrasts with the use of occupation in Western sociological studies. Thus, income and occupation, which have a much narrower range in the modern nation than in the less developed nation, have been shown to have value in certain kinds of political studies. See Robert E. Aggar and Vincent Ostrom, "Political Participation in a Small Community", in *Political Behavior*, Heinz Eulau, ed., Glencoe, Free Press, 1956, pp. 138-148.

preferences that are consistent with their roles as full time, devoted party militants. In ranking the selections concerning national unity in the future, the unoccupied consider recovery of national frontiers of primary importance. Both the modern and traditional occupational groups consider the frontiers question to be of secondary importance to ending unemployment. In ranking the choices concerning the past performance of the government the unoccupied stress the economy, however, while the other two occupational groups rank judicial reforms first. These two groups also rank Morocco's experimental Consultative Assembly lower than the unoccupied group does.

The unoccupeid official expressed especially revealing opinions on the party. Regarding the Istiqlal's future nationally the unoccupied secretaries, and also the traditionally occupied, tended to confuse party and governmental affairs. These two groups placed the economy first, but the modern group appeared to discriminate between party and government more carefully, placing party organizational activity in first place. A similar trend is apparent in the estimates of the Istiqlal's future locally. The unoccupied group thought that promoting large scale national reforms was of primary importance, but the modern group took a more restricted view. To them the important local problems in the future were recruiting more members and solidarity in the face of opposition party threats. Although the results are fragmentary, they display some regularity in portraying the unoccupied group as those most strongly oriented to the party. Their thinking seems to embrace the nationalist cause indiscriminately. Party and nation appear to be equated, and even the local party functions are associated with the furtherance of nationally oriented and nationally supported activity. These preferences are certainly consistent with Chapter II, which suggests that the Istiqlal has developed a number of highly disciplined and totally committed officials.

Educational background is associated with less agreement, and the opinions expressed in reference to educational differences are revealing. In the national and governmental framework the groups with elementary and secondary tend to distinguish themselves from those attending Muslim universities. In the universities Muslim jurisprudence is studied carefully, and it is, therefore, understandable that the university group considered judicial reform to be more important than forming a national army. The university graduates, many of whom are undoubtedly associates of Al-Fassi, place Morocco's irredentist goals above ending un-

133

employment in the future. Their concern with legal reform is carried over into their opinions on the government. They rank the government's past performance in judicial reform, which has been distinguished, of first order importance, and the experimental Assembly second. The efforts to bolster the Moroccan economy are ranked third, although both of the other two educational groups consider the economy most important. Thus, the university educated reveal more concern with the issues that have very likely been stressed in their higher education, and they appear to be more influenced by the historic leader of the Istiqlal, Allal Al-Fassi, himself a Qarawiyn professor and instigator of the frontiers issue.

The group with elementary education differs from the other educational groups largely by its views on the party's role. In judging the party's future nationally the less educated give primary importance to economic improvement. They appeared to be aware of their material interests, and ranked land reform higher than the other two occupational groups for its contribution to national unity in the past. When considering problems of government those with less education ranked the national unity selection lower than the other two groups, and also ranked the irredentist goal lower in considering national goals. Those with some advanced education felt that economic affairs ranked third in the party's future nationally, and gave first preference to party organization. The findings are by no means conclusive, but they suggest that it is not the totally untutored official who is most susceptible to extremist appeals. Those with elementary education can distinguish their material interest and give it preference. They do not emphasize the more emotional nationalist issues as much as do the officials with more education.

Although there is not enough space to relate all the preferences in equal detail, the opinions begin to reinforce earlier conclusions. For example, those who felt fully prepared for their present and higher positions were seen to be generally more experienced in Chapter V. Persons falling into the group of experienced party cadre appeared to be more highly oriented to the party, rather like the unoccupied occupational group with which they overlap. Thus, in judging national unity in the future, the fully prepared official placed the irredentist goal first, while those expressing less confidence placed it second. In considering the future of the government the fully confident ranked the experimental Assembly fifth, while the newly formed representative group was ranked third by others. The more experienced group also ranked the new Assembly lower in reference to the government's past performance. The fully prepared seemed to discriminate between party concerns and government. They ranked party organization first among the Istiqlal's national goals in the future, while those feeling totally unprepared ranked organization third. The unprepared thought the economy was the first national concern of the party, although this responsibility rests clearly with the government. Thus, there are cumulative indications that there are important differences in the official's understanding of politics and his conception of the party's role. The present findings are by no means complete, but they suggest avenues for further inquiry and highlight some of the problems of the lower level Istiqlal officials.

The occurrence of more disagreement in the party and government frameworks has some immediate value in trying to understand some practical problems of nations. First, if the leaders of a new nation permit or desire a situation such that national affairs are regulated by the articulation of social differences in an orderly manner, there must be some device for working out the relatively greater degree of disagreement. The nations generally lack the institutions whereby this is done, as well as the multiplicity of parties that might serve to moderate differences of opinion. Second, the relatively low level of institutional development also means that it is difficult to extend the kind of discussion and decision-making represented by the more immediate frameworks to the entire population. Even nationalist parties are often exclusive organizations when judged by the size of a population. Third, a particular pattern of agreement that might lead to desirable action may rest on kinds of differentiation that are themselves widely objected to. For example, there are several instances where educational differentiation produces disagreement, but any utilization of such views in the political system is limited by other values attached to education and, thereby, by possible charges of favoritism, etc.

Although it may sound odd to say that consensus may be characterized by the high frequency of disagreement, this seems likely when the meaning of the coefficient is explored. Consensus in advanced and less advanced systems may rest on the multiplicity of frameworks and social differentiations through which disagreement is expressed. Consensus does not mean that everyone can agree on one course of action, but that many persons can live together in one political system while disagreeing about many things and in many ways. The new nation that wishes to construct some of the West's capacity to disagree constructively might be well advised to note that such a capacity is elicited by bringing national affairs close to the participants' frame of reference. Although the data does not extend to these questions, it appears likely that when this is done less intense feelings are associated with differences of opinion and also that the more complex pattern of differences makes for greater flexibility in national affairs in general. Politicians are well aware that it is much less disruptive to change one's course of action when there are some persons prepared to subscribe to an alternative course. Moderation in national politics means in part, the ability to make minor adjustments frequently, rather than violent shifts sporadically.

XI

From Nationalism to Nationhood

During the first post-war decade we saw little of the potential schisms and conflicts within the growing nationalist tide, although there were momentary revelations from time to time.[1] The fragmentary knowledge accumulated in that period, the difficulty of conducting more systematic careful study of critically important groups that were already viewed with suspicion, and the general lack of interest in the emerging nations meant that we tended to form and to apply some very misleading simplifications. There was, in fact, little opportunity to test our earlier ideas against past experience because the colonialist experience of the interwar period was so different. The reassertion of British, French, and later Axis supremacy in the undeveloped portion of the world did not permit the kind of rapid political change we are now observing. The Wafd in Egypt and the Congress Party in India, for example, simply lacked the opportunities for success and expansion that the nationalist party enjoyed since 1945. This is partly because of the world scene, but also

---

[1] There have been several such occasions in the history of North African nationalism. One was the thinly concealed resentment of the North African nationalist leaders over the very cool reception they received from the Arab League in the mid-1940's. See Allal Al-Fassi, *The Independence Movements of French North Africa*, (trans. by Hazem Zaki Nuseibeh), Washington, D.C., American Council of Learned Societies, 1954, pp. 378-79 and 402-03. In the post-independence period, differences were once more much in evidence when Bourguiba removed the Bey in 1956, which was regarded as very unfriendly toward the Moroccan and Lybian monarchs, and more recently Bourguiba's dispute with Nasser and avoidance of the new grouping of neutralist Africa states in the 1960 Casablanca meeting.

137

because of increased communications capabilities and knowledge accumulated from the experience of the early colonies. The difficulty of making such comparisons is no doubt one of the major reasons we have so frequently failed to understand nationalism since World War II.

For the above reasons there are several benefits to be derived from a closer examination of the internal affairs of a contemporary nationalist party, which the previous chapters have tried to provide. It is possibly crucial to the success of democracy that we correctly interpret problems of attitudinal and social change in Africa and Asia. We must, first, be able to make policy decisions and formulations that will be understood and effective. Even more important, we must learn in a fairly short space of time what these people are like and how our political system relates to theirs. On the whole the Western world has been slow, and sometimes almost disinterested, in convincing the leaders of the new states that our social adaptibility and psychological flexibility is attainable and appropriate for developing countries. Our inability to do so stems in part from limited knowledge about much of our own behavior. More systematic detailed knowledge must be formulated for comparing and investigating the experience of widely differing cultures. In its most weighty terms the problem involves the reappraisal of most, if not all, the concepts and theories used in the study of Western societies, while we simultaneously embark on the search for new theory and new techniques for the study of wholly unfamiliar problems.

The foregoing chapters are rudimentary, but it is worth summarizing what seems to have been accomplished in reference to the major variables that formed the theme of the chapters. It must be understood, of course, that the conclusions are limited not only by the problems of evaluating the data, but also by limitations in the range of observation. Little can be said, for example, about those with advanced education because, first, very few respondents had a university education and, second, none were from European universities. We have only fragmentary knowledge of how advanced educational groups acquire political roles in the new nations. The growth of human knowledge is to some extent a function of our ability to define problems in new terms and make the required observations. This is clearly the case in our inquiry into the experience of the underdeveloped nations where we must allow for ranges of variation and particular limitations that have seldom been encountered in Western development. It is hoped that some of the exploratory studies herein will facilitate and encourage more systematic inquiry into developing nations.

In several respects the pattern of occupational differences in Chapter II runs counter to that which is frequently assumed to exist in nationalist movements. The Istiqlal had a large quotient of traditionally occupied leaders, of whom its foremost leader, Allal Al-Fassi, was an *alim* of the Muslim university at Fes. This has created a rather misleading image of the nationalists as a collection of Muslim scholars and their devout followers. The occupational characteristics of the party's cadre are a convincting demonstration of the movement's complexity. The modern occupational groups were the first to join the party, and dominate its organization in the advanced provinces. Such secretaries may, of course, be perfectly devout Muslims, but they are also detached in the sense that their livelihoods are derived from something other than religious vocations. These were, in fact, the persons who had the skills and resources needed to organize and sustain a nationwide party. It is often forgotten that next to Allal Al-Fassi and his colleagues from Fes, the most important leaders were from the merchant families of Casablanca, Rabat, and Salé. Large numbers of traditionally occupied became local officials only in 1956, when independence had already been achieved and the party faced the problem of finding officials for a much larger organization. Even so, persons in modern occupations tended to fill the critical organizational positions, while the traditionally occupied were more often found in the retarded provinces and almost never in the cities.

Those with traditional occupational background are most likely the least influential persons in the party. They are the oldest of the occupational groups and have the least confidence in themselves. They also display more aspiration for advancement and may be a source of tension. Although fervent in their religious self-estimates, they did not manage to participate in the resistance in large numbers because of the sheer physical barriers to traditionally occupied persons joining and working in the resistance. Be that as it may, it also means that they are not qualified by what has come to be one of the most important standards of patriotism. The traditionally occupied are, therefore, possibly an imminent source of discontent.[2] Although visited frequently by the inspec-

---

2 The contrast with the more confident, better established occupational categories

tors and generally promoted more rapidly than their colleagues in the more highly organized parts of the country, they lack the qualifications for rapid self-improvement and for special treatment. Since they control the more remote, rural segment of the party structure they have more influence in the long run development of the Istiqlal than they realize.

Perhaps the most intriguing speculation for the future centers on the unoccupied category. There seems to be little doubt, both from the data and the author's field work, that the Istiqlal had an "inner core" of supported officials. In some respects they are the equivalent of the ward-heelers and patronage seekers found in parties of Western countries. They had a high resistance record, and do not share the fervency of the traditionally occupied. They are on the whole younger, concentrated more heavily at the section level of office, and took office sooner than the other occupational groups. Their experience in previous office and long party history must make them extremely valuable officials, although the data collected to test effectiveness in office did not prove reliable. The Istiqlal's future problem is how to support these persons as the government and administration becomes increasingly separated from the nationalist party. The close ties of the past have been dissolved and for much of 1959 the Istiqlal was not active in the King's cabinet. By 1963 policy differences between the Palace and the Istiqlal finally drove the nationalist party into open opposition. The privileges and sinecures that probably provided support for the unoccuied will come more and and more under royal scrutiny and access will be demanded by other parties.

The internal problems of the Istiqlal appear in dramatic form in the analysis of educational differentiation in Chapter III. The educationally less privileged have on the whole had about an equal chance of taking higher office as those whose education recommends them much more highly. It is not entirely clear to what extent this is because of the scarci-

---

is obvious, and suggests that more than ordinary caution should be exercised in evaluating the volatile state of mind of the tribesman. He is no doubt under severe tension as he sees his way of life eroded by modern influence, but it is not the same attitudinal problem as that of the unoccupied party official, for example, who has a deep affective attachment to national ideals and expresses specific national opinions. For those interested in political development, there are important attitudinal differences between conflict resulting from an inability to relate one's self to change and from an emotional identification with the nation as it actually exists.

ty of trained officials or because of the party's failure to promote and encourage better qualified members. It is probably the former since there was a heavy influx of less educated in 1956 and 1957, most of them with only elementary education. Such secretaries are generally aware that they are less well prepared, although their awareness does not seem to reduce their aspirations to organizational advancement. Those who are better prepared but lack party experience, on the other hand, seem to have expectations and self-evaluations that are more harmonious with their capabilities. In any event, the analysis suggests the internal dilemmas that growing nationalist movements must regularly encounter.

Once again some of our commonly held assumptions about educational differentiation are shown to be open to question, or, at least, in need of more empirical investigation. The person with advanced education is not the ascetic or the recluse, but appears to be very like his counterpart in other parts of the world. The well educated person in the party is very likely to be more linguistically accomplished and seldom has a Berber background. Through his memberships he is solidly integrated into the surrounding social structure, which is generally advanced and complex where he is found. He may be tempted to neglect his party duties, or to put them into perspective with other activity in a way that the less advanced citizen might not. His ability to do so is very likely one of the contributing characteristics of the more moderate, more specialized kind of political system associated with modern social structure. Although the data does not permit firm conclusions, there is at least the possibility that the range of social differentiation may be increasing, rather than decreasing, during some phases of a new nation's development. If new activity is largely supervised by and occupied with the concerns of the few who have special educational privilege, those who are struggling to improve themselves may feel that independence has only brought bitter fruit in the form of a new team of superior and inaccessible persons.

More work is also needed in the crucial middle range of educational achievement. National development will begin to increase the numbers of persons having secondary education. In the party they appear to be aware of their comparative inadequacy and may well be more desperate and determined than those whose lack of opportunity has restricted their understanding of a better world. It seems possible that the intermediate educational group tends to be less tolerant and more impatient, rather like some upward mobile groups in Western societies. Those with secondary education display the highest aspirations of any educational group, and they are also the youngest. They also have the highest confidence in their preparation for their present and higher office. In many ways they are more exclusively oriented to the party than the more privileged, although the intermediate educational group also joins many organizations. It seems that they may provide fertile ground for absolutist political thinking, but certainly not necessarily Communist thinking. But those with secondary education, like those in the unoccupied occupational group, have expectations, fortunes, and memories more closely tied to the struggle for independence than any other group. At the same time they lack the moderating influence of age, long experience, and developed alternative interests.

The study of language differentiation in Chapter IV indicates the need to reconsider our conception of the importance of language in Morocco and possibly in other developing nations. The most important immediate result of the analysis is to show that where other circumstances are equal the Berber speaking official is very like any other official. The differences that once existed among the linguistic groups of Morocco have, of course, been lost through generations of war, migration and invasion. The Berber speaking officials show that they have certain handicaps as a result of their social isolation. The most severe difficulty of the Berber speaking person is advancing educationally, although there has been some compensation in the form of occupational advancement. Even where the Berber speaking party official acquires more education he may harbor some ill-feeling toward privileged groups because he is often older before he acquires higher status.

There may well be a critical phase in the social development of those who have been isolated and to some extent neglected because of language differences. The rurally based political party, the Popular Movement, has in fact probably benefited from such differences. It is to be hoped, however, that immediate political gains will not lead Moroccans into attaching lasting significance and magnified importance to differences that are only part of a passing phase in an inescapable process of social development and integration. Although the Istiqlal may appear to be the antagonist in some ways, it should also be acknowledged that the party has been instrumental in bringing the various linguistic groups

together and welding them into one organization. Where the language difference is still important it works to the advantage of the Berber speaking official as well as to his disadvantage. The Berber speaking official has had roughly the same access to higher positions in the party, even though he may not wield the influence of more accomplished local officials. The Istiqlal must have a truly national organization in order to fulfill its claims to pre-eminence, and the process of doing this has led the party to make its contribution to eliminating the significance of language differences.

Not only has the party needed some persons with skill in Berber dialects, but it has also needed more bilingual officials. In many respects the most successful official is bilingual. He has had the best chances for promotion, and is generally better accomplished in terms of other demographic variables for a variety of converging reasons. His importance is underscored by the evidence that the party official who knows only classical Arabic in addition to Maghrebi has not done well in the party organization. He has less chance of taking higher office, is generally confined to the cities and seems to avoid certain kinds of activities. Certainly more inquiry is needed concerning the thinking of this minority, who also have claims to prestige and distinction in the past. The charge has been made, of course, that the Istiqlal is dominated by Arab families who share the orthodox Muslim habits of this kind of secretary, but the Istiqlal has been compelled to make way for all linguistic groups whether high officials approve of them or not. The party would be doomed if it were to allow itself to become the instrument of such a small minority and on the basis of such insignificant, transitory differentiation.[3]

More crucial questions for the party, and also for the country, are raised by the inquiry into the confidence and aspirations of the secretaries in Chapter V. Although it would be risky to make sweeping generalizations, research has demonstrated that general attitudes of this

---

[3] The 1963 elections for the Moroccan National Assembly indicate that a different pattern may emerge. Under King Hassan II a royalist front received the support of the Popular Movement, and strong support from the tribal areas. Although the Istiqlal was in opposition, it managed to receive about a fourth of the seats. However, the alliance of less advanced regions with the Palace present as new alignment which is potentially as divisive as an Istiqlal alignment.

kind affect a wide range of behavior.[4] Evaluations made within the party framework may well be expressed in similar situations. The inquiry was particularly fruitful in demonstrating what might be called the discontinuities in the ambitions and evaluations of the new citizen. Like the new nation as a whole, the nationalist party is a rapidly changing frame of reference in the post-independence period. The organization is relatively new and is itself in the course of making adjustments to independence. As a result the Istiqlal, and very likely other institutions, are not able to provide a stable focus for individual needs and aspirations. They do not appear to serve as focal points as the individual tries to orient himself to the political system and to other questions in this society. There are, in an almost literal sense, no fixed points, psychologically speaking. The party officials did not evaluate their organizations as having defined, generally agreed upon significance, which may and may not correspond to the actual state of affairs in different parts of the new country.

Perhaps the most persuasive evidence in this regard is the failure of confidence of preparation for present or higher office to correlate with level of office. Organizational distinction did not have consistent meaning, but confidence was bolstered by having held office previously. The latter observation suggests the situation is not totally unstructured. There are some identifiable criteria for establishing confidence, although they are not necessarily related to time in office or time in the party. The act of recognition of having attained office seems to be the crucial step in establishing confidence. Living in cities, which may tend to bolster the general confidence level, also tends to create party officials who view their skills optimistically. It is extremely important that more be learned about how confidence and self-reliance are created in the political life of the developing nation.

---

[4] The theoretical foundations have been laid in M. J. Rosenberg's "A Structural Theory of Attitudinal Change," *Public Opinion Quarterly*, v. 24, 1960, pp 319-340; and also the book done by Rosenberg and his associates, *Attitude Orrganization and Change: An Analysis of Consistency Among Attitude Components*, New Haven, Yale University Press, 1960. Similar suggestions, which have important applications to attitudinal change in developing countries, have been made by N. Maccoby and E. E. Maccoby, "Homeostatic Theory in Attitude Change," *Public Opinion Quarterly*, v. 25, 1961, pp. 538-545; and by I. Sarnoff and D. Katz, "The Motivational Bases of Attitude Change," *Journal of Abnormal and Social Psychology*, v. 49, 1954, pp. 115-124.

As such inquiries continue, one intriguing, but possibly misleading, aspect of the study seems most pertinent. The expression of confidence may be informed and articulate or it may be simply a vague, embracing feeling that things must get better. It is not too surprising that both types of confidence were probably elicited in the widely differentiated sample being studied. The generally less prepared and less advanced official often expressed aspirations and self-evaluations that were equal to or surpassed those of the better qualified secretary. Thus, those who lacked confidence and also had held less previous office had a level of aspiration equal to those who felt confidence and had had office previously. In some distributions it appeared that those who were in fact less privileged and less qualified were attaching particularly high hopes to the party. Those with less education and less occupational status had higher aspirations than others. Feeling unprepared for office and having the handicap of being in a less advanced province also results in higher aspirations. The Istiqlal may be hard put to fulfill such expectations, but they illustrate how the major nationalist organization may become the most important reference group for attitudinal and social change. The important difference between the new nation and the more advanced nation is that the nationalist party encounters endless material obstacles, and may turn to purely emotional, highly affective issues in order to create rewards. What the Istiqlal has contributed by integrating some of the least privileged Moroccans into political life may be sacrificed when attitudinal rigidities are introduced at a slightly later phase in order to distract the ambitious militant from the deprivations and hardships of national reconstruction. In this regard, it is important to note that those subscribing most enthusiastically to the extreme national unity theme were socially advanced, but politically less experienced.

Although not as subject to distortion and abuse as linguistic differentiations, religious differences are of historic importance in every Muslim country, and much theorizing in politics contains explicit or implicit assumptions about the kind of attitudes presumably fostered by Islam. More systematic research into the relationship of Islam and national politics is just beginning, but the analysis given in Chapter VI suggests some of the mistakes that might very easily be made and perpetuated. One of the major errors stems from the widely held view that the Istiqlal, having important origins in religious reform of Islam, is a party

145

especially devoted to religion *per se*.[5] Its leaders may hold these views and the members may agree on religious doctrine but its local officials represent a wide variety of religious sentiment in everyday life. Religious sentiment does not correlate with level of office. Although more religious persons tended to take more high office at an early period of Istiqlal history, this trend has been reversed in the post-independence period. Now the more religious official is more likely to be a recent recruit and become a sub-section official. This is a function of the party's historical situation since it did attract religious reformers initially and made religious reform one of its early purposes. Today the party must adjust to new national and organization needs, and operate in a political environment in which religious sentiments are so mixed that they fail to establish any clear differences among party officials.

In the post-World War II period the Istiqlal recruited and trained its first large cadre, and in doing so appears to have admitted many persons who had more immediate goals than religious reform. They are, in general, the persons who have led the split from the party, and who are supported by the trade unions. But a new group of more religious persons were admitted since independence, who are differentiated from their predecessors by being more concentrated in the remote parts of the country, by having less education, and by having very little party experience. These new religious persons are concentrated at the sub-section level of office and have become an integral part of the post-independence party organization. The recently recruited religious secretaries also tend to be older, as new local officials in the more remote parts of the country are very likely to be. Most of the young persons with some training and talent, who tend to consider themselves less religious, move to cities and urban centers where there are more opportunities.

---

[5] This is typical of the kind of easy simplification that may be made when speaking of Islam in very broad terms. Psychologically, the monarch's committment to the religion is very different from that of the nationalist elders. As *immam* the king can reconstruct his image while avoiding committment to specific national issues, but the nationalists' religious claims need some specific attachment, such as irredentist campaign to convey their devotion to Islam and to enable them, in turn, to exploit religious feelings for political purposes. Al-Fassi may be more intense in his Islamic sentiments, though no more devoted than the king. This is to some extent born out in the Istiqlal leader's willingness to part from the king over issues attached to an Islamic revival.

This entire situation puts the Istiqlal, and probably many other national-ist movements in transition, in a very difficult position.

High aspirations for party advancement are expressed by the more religious regardless of experience in previously holding office, while the less experienced and less religious tend to acknowledge their relative handicap. The correlation has several implications, which are generally borne out by other psychological studies.[6] The party officials most strongly affected by Islamic notions express extreme views in several ways. They are less cognizant of their own inadequacies, while placing more absolute demands on the country in terms of irredentism and rapid Moroccanization. Thus, one can detect attitudinal consistency among the more devout, but accompanied with a less accurate perception of both the individual's situation and Morocco's international position. Without more data it is difficult to estimate the burdens placed on the party leaders by extremist attitudes. Certainly the party split in 1959 came about in part as a result of the party elders' insistence on unreal-istic goals, which eventually even broke the Istiqlal away from the mon-archy. The difficulties of national reconstruction have led many political forces in Morocco, including the King, to rely more heavily on highly affective appeals. As the inconsistency mounts, it seems likely that at-titudinal coherence is maintained only by introducing perceptual rigidi-ties and new inflammatory stimuli. Such a setting is hardly appropriate for the prosaic, tedious tasks of national development.[7]

The pattern of religious differentiation sheds some light on the divi-

---

[6] Until recently, most of the studies appropriate to the attitudinal problem raised here have been in the United States and in laboratories. However, we have a much clearer notion of how the individual seeks to reconcile affective and cognitive components of his perceptual world as a result of the researches cited above. These more elaborate, and therefore more useful, theories stem from earlier works on cognitive dissonance by F. Heider, T. M. Newcomb, C. E. Osgood, P. H. Tannen-baum, and Leon Festinger.

[7] There are some interesting problems connected with the obvious attractiveness of labor-investment programs, advocated most energetically by the Chinese Com-munists, but also present in our own Food for Peace proposals. These are develop-mental devices that require less understanding of the overall significance of the changes effected, and that hold great appeal to leaders and groups hoping to trans-form the new nation by the continued exploitation of affective appeals. These no-tions have been put forth more regularly by continental writers. See, for example, René Dumont, *Terres Vivantes*, Paris, Editions Plon, 1961. Some of the political implications of such development are being explored in a study now under way by the author.

sion of the nationalist movement. Even more helpful in this regard was the analysis of the resistance experience. The Istiqlal has failed almost uniformly to persuade resistance members to join the party who did not belong to the party before independence. The people in the party who went into the resistance were among the earily recruits, but neither auxiliary associations nor the party were successful in bringing into the Istiqlal persons who joined the resistance during the struggle. The resistance, of course, had its own organization and had its own avenues of expression through contacts with the King. However, the discontent must have been profound. Both new parties, the Popular Movement, and the new National Union formed from the Istiqlal splinter group, had among their most prominent officers leading resistance figures. The violent experience of the independence struggle has left its mark on the Istiqlal in other ways. Like the country as a whole, the party is indebted to the resistance members, who are concentrated in the more advanced provinces. Party officials without resistance experience are concentrated in the remote, less advanced provinces, where the need for substantial support distributed as veterans' relief is also great. Since the distribution of veterans' benefits was taken over by the Palace, the conflict has been minimized.

By their tentative nature the attitudinal chapters are more difficult to summarize, although they do touch on several points of continuing interest in the study of attitude formation in developing countries. As Professor McClelland's work has pointed out[8] there is evidence that persons undergoing major attitudinal transformation are first affected by very general notions and values that may be injected into their perceptual environment in a variety of ways. The Istiqlal has undoubtedly been one of the most important Moroccan organizations re-orienting attitudes and opinions to the tasks of nation-building. The party's role is enhanced as more studies into similar problems of national integration underscore the importance of national values not only as mobilizing stimuli, but as devices essential to the conceptual re-organization of a previously simplified world. National values are not only a reservoir of emotional, patriotic energy, but they help the new citizen organize a more complex perceptual world and attach cognitive meaning to new events and relationships.

---

[8] *The Achieving Society*, Princeton, Van Nostrand, 1961.

148

When the analyses of the unity theme and opposition tolerance, presented in Chapters VIII and IX, are viewed as a whole, the emergent attitudes among local officials do not appear to encourage moderate, sustained political development. The vicissitudes of the independence struggle combined with embittered party relations since 1956 have led the local militants to stress national unity. Relatively few appear to perceive the local community's relation to national affairs, or to allow for the moderating effects of social and personal differences in political life. In terms of the growth of the Istiqlal there appear to be three major categories of party secretaries. There are, first, the original militants, whose party affiliation dates back to the 30's. Their prestige within the party and the social privilege which enabled them to become active political participants so early in the Istiqlal's history make them a peculiar group. Not only are they confident officials, but they also reflect their exposure to Western ideals before relations with the colonial tutor became exacerbated. They are less extremist in both analyses, being more tolerant of opposition parties and less attracted to the emotional issues of Moroccan politics. They appear able to absorb a variety of information, enjoy a relatively complex pattern of social relationships, and in the whole are content with the party as it is. Although an influential group in party politics, they are also a vanishing minority in Moroccan political life and probably find it hard to withstand pressure from the more numerous, more extreme party secretaries.

There is secondly a group of "hard line" local officials, who are most likely typical of local nationalist officials. They are psychologically hardened in the sense that they are more dependent on the party for psychic rewards and social satisfactions than either the elders or the newer secretaries. For example, they can withstand the conflict of witnessing democratic practices within the party, while denying the applicability of such practices in situations where the opposition might gain. Although some hard line secretaries concede a meaningful role to the opposition, they tend to reduce the role where more opposition party activity is indeed encountered. The more severe local official is found in the more advanced provinces, was generally recruited into the party during the more intense struggle from 1947 to 1952, and tends to be more dependent on party life.

The last phase of organizational expansion, largely since independence, has introduced a fairly large proportion of less skilled, less confi-

149

dent party officials into the Istiqlal. They tend to be more remote from moder nlife spatially, by being concentrated in the previously less organized remote provinces, and socially, by being located in areas with less group activity oriented to specific needs and interests. In many ways the new officials are still so rooted in tradition, reflected by their Koranic educations and party histories, that the problem of attitudinal reconciliation may not be as pressing. Quite possibly they tend to adopt modern attitudes in a ritualistic way, even to the extent of expressing approval of institutions and practices with little understanding of their significance in national politics. Because the less experienced party seccretary may tend to copy those attitudes he thinks appropriate to national politics, the consistency he sometimes expresses in taking less extreme positions in regard to the opposition and the unity theme may not represent an attitude rooted in his personal life or even his community, where opinions on national events and problems are very likely rudimentary and fragmented.

Considering how little we know of relatively basic attitudinal components in developing countries, it is perhaps ambitious to think simultaneously on problems of attitudinal structure or integration. However, our investigations into the opinions, feelings and sentiments of the citizen of the developing country, and how such elements are attitudinally reconciled, should benefit from similar studies in other countries. The purpose of more systematic inquiry is, in part, to make possible such transfer of method and theory. Chapter X raised some of these considations in the analysis of consensus formation among the party officials. Since many political participants in the countries of Africa and Asia are only now formulating views suited to problems and opportunities presented by the modern nation, it is conceivable that furthei investigation along these lines may contribute to our understanding of the more complex attitudinal structures constructed by the citizen of more privileged societies.

The findings presented in Chapter X can be interpreted either as an expression of agreement or disagreement, although it has been argued that more can be learned from the character of the differences expressed in Table X-1. Issues and problems were least differentiated in relation to explicit social differences, e.g., occupation, language and education. Differentiation of rankings also decreased as the framework of evaluation became more remote. It is also pertinent that the range of differentiation was less when the respondents were divided according to social differences rather than more subjective estimates or more general attitudes. The structural feature of particular significance, however, is the tendency to express more difference in evaluating national questions as the framework came closer to the respondent's field of experience. The chances that a person can take action or seek relief are, of course, relatively greater in the more familiar setting and better known environment. Part of the success of democratic government, as well as more productive economic system generally, seems to be their suitability for localizing problems, and centering popular attention on attitudinal dimensions that do not correspond to intensely felt differences. The horizontal axis of the table has similar meaning, in demonstrating that consensus decreases as more general ideas are introduced into the respondent's perceptual framework, or as self-estimates involving personal considerations and other more tense relationships are introduced. Methodologically, the chapter supports those inquiries suggesting that consensus can be more readily grasped by studying the nature of our disagreement, especially where we are dealing with the large range of social and personal differences found in the developing country. Maximum consensus may mean social stagnation and individual inadaptibility.[9]

The developing countries are fascinating laboratories for the study of attitudinal formation. The interest in authoritarian personality and its relation to politics in the more advanced countries has, to some extent, created more interest in the affective, extremist components of more complex attitudes, but the new country also presents opportunity to explore the cognitive aspect of attitudes as new citizens are asked to play more important roles in national reconstruction. It may be appropriate that we address ourselves to such problems for the results help us to see how our own values may relate to new patterns of behavior in developing countries, and also because the developing country seldom has time and skill to devote to the more theoretical aspects of social change.[10] In this way more systematic research may contribute to our

---

[9] Although concerned mostly with one aspect of attitude formation, and with the Hagen, *On the Theory of Social Change*, Homewood, Dorsey Press, 1962, has particular relevance.

[10] See Paul Neurath, "Social Research in Newly Independent Countries: An Indian Example," *Public Opinion Quarterly*, v. 24, 1960, pp. 670-674; and also Bruce L. Smith, "Communications Research in Non-Industrial Countries," *Public Opinion Quarterly*, v. 16, 1953, pp. 527-538.

understanding of important social problems of all societies, while contributing to the development of the less advanced nations.

Appendixes

Appendix I: Questionnaire

COVER LETTER

Office of the Istiqlal Party,
Baab al-Ahad
Rabat

5 April 1958

Secretary for Social Research

Praise God,

To secretaries of sections and sub-sections:

You certainly know the great effort of the party to improve its organization and its method of work in order to be able to accomplish its mission of education and orientation, and also to become an instrument for the consolidation of independence after having been an instrument to combat colonialism and to achieve independence.

The meetings of the secretaries of sections and sub-sections with the inspector have multiplied in order to find in common a better way to achieve the party's purpose. Since the declaration of independence we have not known definitely the reforms that circumstances require in the *Bulletin of the Party* (*Nushra al-Hizb*), the work of the cells and the sections, and the organizations attached to the party.

But one should know from one moment to the next the results that we have obtained and be sure that we move progressively as we have planned. This work should be done with the consultation of those who perform this work at the base and with concern for the information furnished us.

Such are the reasons for the questions sent to you and to which we have asked you to respond with precision and clarity. You should fill the blanks before each question with an adequate reply in the attached copies.

You are asked to reply promptly and to put the two copies in the attached envelope and to seal it with the stamp of the section in order that the envelope will not be opened except at the central party office.

We are sure that you will give this task all the interest which it merits and conclude with the wish that you help us.

Muhammad Benchekroun

Note: The envelope should be sent to the inspector in order that he may send them to the central office unopened.

PARTY ORGANIZATION

Note: Most questions are directed to secretaries of sub-sections and sections. In case the question relates to only one, please note. If the question is related to one, then answer in relation to your position and district.

155

1. If you are a secretary of a section, check here ─────.
   If you are a secretary of a sub-section, check here ─────.
2. Location of section or sub-section:
   a. If you are in a town, write its name ───── and province ─────.
   b. If you are in the country, write name of douar ───── and province ─────.
      Write name of tribal fraction ─────.
      Write name of tribe ─────.
3. If you are a sub-section secretary in the city name the section to which you belong ─────.
   If you are a sub-section secretary in the country name the tribal section to which you belong ─────.
   If you are a section secretary name the inspectorate of the party to which your section belongs ─────.
   How many sub-sections are attached to your section? ─────.
4. When was your sub-section organized? Month ───── Year ─────.
   If you are a section secretary when was your section organized?
   Month ───── Year ─────.
5. How many cells were there under your direction in:
   a. January, 1958 ─────.
   b. January, 1957 ─────, or none.
   c. January, 1956 ─────, or none.
   d. Between December 1952* and the summer of 1955 ─────, or none.
   e. Before December 1952* ─────, or none.
6. How many members were there in the district under your administration? (Definition of a member: carried membership card after independence; taken oath; pays dues if in the city; attends cell meetings regularly and acts in the party's favor regularly.)
   a. January 1958 ─────.
   b. January 1957 ─────, or none.
   c. January 1956 ─────, or none.
   d. Between December 1952* and the summer of 1955 ─────, or none.
   e. Before December 1952* ─────, or none.
7. How many members under your administration? ─────.
8. What is the number of members now under your administration that are considered as militants (faithful ones)? (Definition of a militant: attends cell meetings regularly; pays dues; volunteers for party work in his leisure; accepts bearing responsibility.) ─────.
9. What is the population in the district of your section? ─────.
10. What is the number of those who are favorably inclined toward the party? (Definition of a sympathizer (affectionate one): not a member of the

---

* Asterisks in the questionnaire represent translation errors, which have been corrected here. Since the questions were often excessively detailed, the lost data were not crucial. See Appendix II.

156

party and not carrying a membership card; supports the party and votes on its behalf in any elections; attends important ceremonies.) ————.

11. If you are a sub-section secretary, how many times has the sub-section committee met in the last six months? ————.
How many of these times did the inspector of the party visit you? ————.
If you are a section secretary, how many times has the section committee met in the last six months? ————.
How many of these times did the inspector of the party visit you? ————.

12. When was the election of officials in your sub-section or section? Month ———— Year ————.

13. How many times have elections been repeated since the establishment of your section or sub-section? ————.

14. Did any member from your section or sub-section attend the party conference in August 1956? Yes / No.
   a. If more than one, how many?————.
   b. Of these persons, how many now hold party positions? ————.

15. Did you receive instructions from the section? Yes / No
How many times per month? ————.
Do you receive instructions from your inspector? Yes / No
How many times per month? ————.

16. What is the number of opposition party members in your district?
   a. Democratic Party of Independence ————.
   b. Liberal Independents ————.
   c. Moroccan Communists ————.
   d. Party of Unity and Independence ————.
   e. Other (name) ————.

17. What is the number of opposition party offices in your district?
   a. Democratic Party of Independence ————.
   b. Liberal Independents ————.
   c. Moroccan Communists ————.
   d. Party of Unity and Independence ————.
   e. Other (name) ————.

18. Did the party inspector visit your section or sub-section during the last six months? Yes / No
If yes, how many times?

19. How many times in the last six months have you discussed the following subjects with the inspector?
   a. explanation of party policy ————.
   b. explanation of government policy ————.
   c. improvement of internal organization of your section ————.
   d. If there were other important subjects, explain them briefly:

20. Evaluate the following written or verbal sources of news. Write "no" in front of those you do not receive. Grade the others you find useful by putting the number "1" by the most important to you; "2" for the one

of secondary importance, and so forth for all that you use.

——— al-Istiqlal   ——— Sahara al Maghrib
——— al-Alam   ——— Mannar al-Maghrib
——— al-Taliâ   ——— Rai al-Amm
——— Nushra al Hizb   ——— Radio Maroc
——— al-Ahd al-Jadiid   ——— Radio Cairo
                                  ——— Radio Tangier
                                  ——— Talks with government officials
                                  ——— Talks with inspector

21. How do party leaders know about the activity of your sections and if you execute their orders? Put "1" in front of the way you think is the most important; "2" for the secondary importance and so forth.
    a. Meetings of sub-section committee.
    b. Meetings of section * committee.
    c. Visits of inspector and high officials to your sub-section or section.
    d. Your written or verbal reports sent directly.
        If there are other ways you think important, explain briefly:

22. How do you think party leaders record your opinions and those of your section and sub-section? Put "1" in front of the way you think is most important; "2" for secondary importance, and so forth.
    a. Meetings of sub-section committee.
    b. Meetings of section committee.
    c. Visits of inspector and high officials to your sub-section or section.
    d. Your written or verbal reports sent directly.
        If there are other ways you think important, explain briefly:

23. Has it been necessary to discharge any members of your section or sub-section? Yes / No
    a. If yes, date of discharge ———.
    b. In a few words reasons for discharge ———.
    c. How did you make this decision? ———.

24. Has it been necessary to take disciplinary action against any members of section or sub-section? Yes / No
    a. If yes, date of punishment ———.
    b. In a few words reasons for punishment ———.
    c. How did you make this decision? ———.

25. Do all your cells have directors (*musiiriin*)? Yes / No
    a. If not, how many cells do not have directors? ———.
    b. How many of these directors have attended the directors' school?——.

26. Is there an illiteracy organization in your district? Yes / No
    a. If yes, how many sections has it? ———.
    b. Date at which it started its activity? ———.
    c. What is the number of participants in this activity? ———.
    d. What is the number of party members of this total? ———.
    e. What is the number of those who have continued their study to the end? ———.

27. Are there union offices in your section or sub-section district? Yes / No
    a. If yes, what is the number of these offices? ———.
    b. Date they were started ————.
    c. What is the number of unionists of the whole population of your district? ————.
    d. From this total number how many are members of the party? ———.
    e. How many times do you consult with union officials in a month?——.

28. Are there youth organizations in your district? Yes / No
    a. If yes, how many members in them? ————.
    b. What is the number of Istiqlal youth who participate? ————.
    c. Write the number of participants and date of establishment of the following youth organizations:
       ———— Hassaniya Scouts
       ———— Youth Hostelers
       ———— Builders of Independence
       ———— Young Moroccan Workers
       ———— Young Moroccan Scholars
       ———— Young Israelites
       ———— Abdullawiya Scouts

29. If a sub-section secretary, are there members of the resistance movement among the members of your sub-section committee? Yes / No
    a. If yes, how many? ————.
    b. Are there members of the Liberation Army among the members of your sub-section committee? Yes / No
    c. If yes, how many? ————. Were they in the Resistance before? Yes / No
    d. What is the total number of members? ————.

30. If a section secretary, are there members of the resistance movement among the members of your section committee? Yes / No
    a. If yes, how many? ————.
    b. Are there members of the Liberation Army among the members of your section committee? Yes / No
    c. If yes, how many? ————. Where they in the resistance movement before? Yes / No
    d. What is the total number of members? ————.

31. Was there activity of the resistance movement or the Army of Liberation in the region of your section or sub-section? Yes / No
    a. If there was activity in your area, write roughly how many times each of the following kinds of activity took place: *
       ———— destruction or burning of crops
       ———— cutting down of trees
       ———— assassination attacks on Moroccan traitors
       ———— assassination attacks on Frenchmen
       Other kinds (specify) ————.

    b. Was there activity of the Liberation Army in the region of your sec-
tion or sub-section: 1955: Yes / No   1956: Yes / No

    c. If there was activity in your area, write roughly how many times
each of the following kinds of activity took place: °
      —————— destruction or burning of crops
      —————— cutting down of trees
      —————— assassination attacks on Moroccan traitors
      —————— assassination attacks on Frenchmen
      Other kinds (specify) ——————.

32. How many hours per month do the directors spend for each of the following activities:

    a. Teaching party principles to new members ——————.

    b. Discussion with present members ——————.

    c. Anti-illiteracy work ——————.

    d. Youth and feminist activities ——————.

    e. Work to help the position of poor people ——————.

    f. If there is something else important, describe it in a few words:

33. How many hours do you as a secretary of a section or a sub-section spend
for each of the following activities per month?

    a. Teaching party principles to new members ——————.

    b. Discussion with present members ——————.

    c. Anti-illiteracy work ——————

    d. Youth and feminist activities ——————.

    e. Work to help the position of poor people ——————.

    f. If there is something else important, describe it in a few words:

34. How many hours does the average member of the party spend for the following activities per month?

    a. Teaching party principles to new members ——————.

    b. Discussion with present members——————.

    c. Anti-illiteracy Work ——————.

    d. Youth and feminist activities ——————.

    e. Work to help the position of poor people ——————.

    f. If there is something else important, describe it in a few words:

35. Do you have consultation with any government officials in your district:
Yes / No

    a. If yes, how many times per month ——————.

    b. What is the position these officials occupy? ——————.

    c. If you had more help from the government, what kind would you
choose? ——————.

    d. Is the caid in the area of your section or sub-section a member of
the Istiqlal? Yes / No

    e. Is the super-caid in the area of your section or sub-section a member
of the Istiqlal? Yes / No

36. Are there sections for women in your section or sub-section? Yes / No

    a. If yes, when were they founded? Month —————— Year ——————.

b. How many women's cells exist now? ————.
c. How many women belong to these cells? ————.
d. How many married women belong to these cells? ————.
e. How many meetings per month of these cells? ————.
f. Are there general meetings for all the women? ————.
g. Estimate the number of women who attend these meetings? ————.
h. Are there the following kinds of activity?

> —————— illiteracy
> —————— social welfare
> —————— Red Crescent
> —————— child care
> —————— help for workers
> —————— cultural club
> —————— sports club

PERSONAL BACKGROUND

1. Year of Birth ————.
2. Place of Birth: If a town, name —————— and province ————. If the country, Douar ————— fraction ————— tribe ————— and province ———.
3. Profession of father ————.
4. Have you any employment in addition to your service in the party?
   Yes / No
   a. If yes, what kind of work? ————.
   b. How many hours does this work take each week? ————.
   c. What is the income from this work? Francs per week: ————.
5. Are you married ————, widower ————, divorced ————, or un-married ————?
6. Years of study in the following schools: Years from — to
   a. village Koranic school (*musiid*)
   b. free school (party)
   c. French-Moroccan school
   d. European school
   e. official school (government)
   f. professional or trade school
   g. others (name)
8. In what month and year did you join the party? Month ——— Year ———.
9. Through which of the following organizations did you first get in touch with the party the first time?
   a. factory or union
   b. Liberation Army or resistance
   c. organized recruitment effort
   d. volunteer
   e. school
   f. Koranic school

10. Write in a few words the reason you joined the party:
11. Did you join the party in your present place of work? Yes / No
12. Give the month and year that you started your present work or office in the party job. Month ————— Year —————.
    a. Have you ever had a job in the party before? Yes / No
    b. If yes, what was this job? —————.
    c. Was this job in the same town and place of work? Yes / No
13. Were you ever imprisoned by French or Spanish authorities? Yes / No
    a. If yes, from what month ————— and year ————— to what month ————— and year?
    b. Were you ever in forced residence by French or Spanish authorities? Yes / No If yes, from what month ————— and year ————— to what month ————— and year —————?
    c. Were you ever imprisioned* by the French or Spanish authorities? Yes / No If yes, from wat month ————— and year ————— to what month ————— and year—————?
    d. Was a brother, father, or son imprisoned by French or Spanish authorities?
    e. Were you ever brutally mistreated by French or Spanish authorities? Yes / No
14. Did you participate in the party's armed resistance before independence? Yes / No
    a. If yes, in the city or in the country?
    b. Were you a member of the Liberation Army? Yes / No
    c. If yes, from what month ————— and year ————— to what month ————— and year —————?
    d. Were you a member of the Resistance Movement? Yes / No
    e. If yes, from what month ————— and year ————— to what month ————— and year —————?
15. Mention the newspapers and periodicals in which you read at least one page or one article in each number:
16. Mention the clubs and organizations in which you participate regularly in addition to your party activity:
17. Were you a member of a union? Yes / No
    a. If yes, name of union and town:
    b. Do you belong to a union now? Yes / No
    c. If yes, name of union and town:
    d. Date of membership: Month ————— and year —————.
    e. Have you ever been a union official? Yes / No
    f. Are you a union official now? Yes / No
18. Did you finish any kind of study to prepare you for your present party job? Yes / No
    a. If yes, was the training in a party cadre school? Yes / No
    b. Period of training: Month ————— and year ————— to Month ————— and year —————.

    c. How many officials of your section or sub-section have had this training? ————.

    d. In what town did you attend a party cadre school? ————.

    e. What subjects was this training about? ————.

    f. In what subjects do you still need training? ————.

19. According to your needs give "1" to the most important subjects "2" for secondary importance and so forth:

    ———— party objectives and program information.

    ———— government problems and projects information.

    ———— directions on party organization and operation.

    ———— directions and program concerning aid to poor people.

    ———— general study of language, history, and geography, etc.

20. Do you think that your study is sufficient for your present job? Yes / No

    a. Do you think it is sufficient for a higher job? Yes / No

    b. Do you wish to have a higher job? Yes / No

21. Can you describe your attitude toward religion?

    ———— fervently religious.

    ———— moderately religious.

    ———— disinterested in religion.

    ———— atheist or agnostic.

    a. How many times do you pray each day? ————.

    b. How many times do you visit the mosque each week? ————.

    c. Do you fast during Ramadan? Yes / Almost always

22. If you are married, did you choose your wife by yourself? Yes / No

    a. If you are not married, do you expect to choose your own wife? Yes / No

    b. Do you believe your wife should remain in the home without outside work? Yes / No

    c. That she may work outside the home? Yes / No

23. Which of the following roles do you think will be useful for opposition parties?

    ———— do nothing that may effect national unity.

    ———— criticize carefully and refuse to build popular support.

    ———— criticize freely and organize small parties.

    ———— use all means to organize large opposition parties.

PREFERENCE RATING QUESTIONS**

** Note: Only the preference questions used in the book have been reprinted. The preference questions did not appear in this order in the questionnaire. Questions 1 through 4 appeared in the order given here. Those numbered 5 and 6 here were 7 and 8; number 7 here was number 5; and number 8 here was number 9.

In the following fifteen questions you will find a problem or situation for which there are five solutions. You are to number and arrange these solutions or opinions, each of which represents a solution or opinion which relates to the problem. Use the number "1" for the solution of the most importance, "2" for second importance, etc., for all five. There is no correct answer, but use your opinion.

1. Give numbers to the following achievements since independence according to the way in which they have contributed to national unity:
   —————— court reform.
   —————— progress of unions.
   —————— land distribution.
   —————— creation of Sureté National and Royal Army.
   —————— establishment of Consultative Assembly and projected elections.

2. Give numbers to the following problems according to the way in which you think they will contribute to national unity in the future:
   —————— ending unemployment and increasing production.
   —————— recovery of Moroccan frontiers.
   —————— reform and increased production in agriculture.
   —————— choosing a National Assembly by elections and giving full rights to its laws.
   —————— training of technicians and civil servants for government projects.

3. Give numbers to the following problems according to your view on how they will be important to the future of the Istiqlal in its national activities:
   —————— economy (industrialization, unemployment, capital).
   —————— politics (election of a National Assembly).
   —————— internal party organization (recruitment, organization, indoctrination).
   —————— social affairs (illiteracy, helping poor, feminist work).
   —————— national unity (opposition threat, reform administration, Moroccanization).

4. Give numbers to the following questions according to the importance for each for the party's future in local activities:
   —————— village projects to help poor people whether or not of the party.

————— admission, indoctrination and organization of party members.

————— explanation of large national reforms and government activities for all.

————— solidarity of the party against opposition parties.

————— understanding of the administration and civil service activities.

5. Give numbers to the success of the government up to the present with the following national questions:

————— economy (industrialization, unemployment, capital).

————— politics (plans for elections, National Assembly).

————— justice (organization of courts, codification of law).

————— social problems (public works, education, public health).

————— national administration (purge, Moroccanization, organization of civil service).

6. Give numbers to the importance of the following national questions in the future in your opinion:

————— economy (industrialization, unemployment, capital).

————— politics (plan for elections, National Assembly).

————— justice (organization of courts, codification of law).

————— social problems (public works, education, public health).

————— national administration (purge, Moroccanization, organization of civil service).

7. Give numbers according to the interest of the members of section and subsections in the following questions:

————— economy (industrialization, unemployment, capital formation).

————— politics (plan for elections, National Assembly).

————— justice (organization of courts, codification of laws).

————— social problems (public works, education, public health).

————— national administration (purge, Moroccanization, organization of civil service).

8. Give numbers to the following factors that have caused difficulties for the members in their section and sub-section activities:

————— insufficient funds.

————— poor help from sympathizers and their lack of concern.

————— existence and activity of opposition party.

————— poor discipline among members.

————— poor planning and help from the government.

Appendix II: Administration Questionnaire

While working on this study several persons expressed an interest in the practical problems of administering a questionnaire in a new nation, and suggested that students of similar interest might benefit from the author's experience. The limitations of the sample have already been stressed in the Introduction and the scoring of the preference questions is given in detail in an article in the *Public Opinion Quarterly*, vol. 25, Spring, 1961, pp. 106-114. This information will not be repeated but the working problems of administering the questionnaire will be outlined. As might be apparent from this inquiry itself, the author is optimistic about the usefulness of survey research in the developing nations, and feels that such research permits us to study many problems that have long been neglected in our inquires into the politics of developing nations.

In political studies both written questionnaires and interviewing will very likely be limited to fairly well structured situatons for some time. Some attempts have been made at random sampling in single villages or sections of an urban *medina*. Although such studies meet generally accepted statistical standards for reliable generalization, they are hard to use in the study of national politics. Most new nations lack sufficient information about their own population to permit selecting and finding anything approaching a nationally based random sample. For political inquiries the alternative is to concentrate on crucial groups within the society which have known parameters. Survey work can be combined with more general studies in such a way to enhance their value, while simultaneously laying groundwork for more ambitious survey research in the future. There are also non-parametric statistical methods to resolve some problems. It must be acknowledged that many problems of political behavior in advanced political systems have been studied under the same limitations. With the exception of the voting studies and a few major sociological studies of political significance, very little survey work has been done on the scale needed to study political behavior at the national level.

In considering the arrangements for survey work in a new nation, it seems advisable to select an organization through which the student can work. This is what has been done in Berger's *Bureaucracy and Society in Modern Egypt*, and Pye's *Guerilla Communism in Malaya*. This means, of course, that friendly governments will be most helpful in this kind of research, but it does not mean that we are barred from studying the kind of problem that we know to exist in

167

less hospitable political systems. Unfortunately, we do not yet have sufficient comparative studies to begin to give some idea of the reproducibility of the results of exploratory studies. It would be most desirable if some attempt was made to collect data on similar problems as survey work proceeds so that we may begin to have the benefit of cumulative findings as well as experience in applying similar methods in varying social situations.

How one establishes confidence in a new nation is a highly personal affair, but it is the first step toward getting official cooperation. The author was especially fortunate in having strong support from several members of the Istiqlal Executive Committee. It should be remembered that political leaders in new nations are usually well aware of their need for more precise information about their people and their country. In certain kinds of political systems, both more or less developed, there are certain risks in permitting the collection and publication of precise information. Even in systems where the leaders encourage systematic study of their country, the results may often be abused by opportunistic politicians or misunderstood by ill-informed persons. However, hesitant officials can often be assured if it is explained that it takes several years to process and evaluate this kind of data, and if it is made clear that the results will be of value to them. How one points up the practical value of the survey naturally depends on the kind of study the student wishes to undertake and the existing situation in the country concerned. As leaders of new nations see the beneficial results of economic and demographic studies it seems likely that more interest will be shown in exploring less concrete problems systematically.

The procedure for assuring constant meaning between English and the language of administration is fairly standard. In this case the author made his own rough translation first. However, unless the student has near perfect knowledge of the local language and its dialectical idiosyncracies outside help is needed. This is not difficult to find, although foreign students sometimes exaggerate their knowledge of English. The author worked with a young civil servant, who made a finished translation into Moroccan Arabic. A professional translator was then paid to make a translation back into English, and appropriate adjustments were made. With this completed translation the author approached friends in the party for a final polishing of terminology and usage. This step varies with the administering agency and kind of problem under study. Political parties often have special terms and standard phrases for their activity and organization.

In this case a small committee was organized to pre-test the questionnaire. The working committee later proved to be more important than the author realized at the time. It contained some officials of different political views, and when the party split a year later it was learned that the members of the working committee on the questionnaire had also divided. Thanks to the unseen guidance of the sponsors on the Executive Committee, who were well aware of growing tensions in the party, the working committee included all viewpoints. This meant that all shades of opinion at party headquarters were reassured that the questionnaire was not a partisan device. Nevertheless, the response from the areas where the party organization was in the hands of older, more conservative officials was poor. This may be accounted for simply by their suspicion of any modern device or their refusal to follow relatively specific orders of this kind. Be that as it may, the working committee gave the author support at headquarters and established friendly relations with the key officials in the administration of the questionnaire.

The author feels that we often permit our unfamiliarity with a foreign setting to handicap establishing friendly relations. It should be remembered that a Western social scientist is as strange to an Arab official as the official is to the new arrival. Furthermore, most officials have respect for American technical competence and skill even if they are doubtful about our foreign policy. Once the questionnaire is explained in understandable terms suspicions may be alleviated and curiosity may be created. A further possible asset on the student's side is that the American scholar is relatively unknown in many new nations, where scholars from the earlier colonial country may be met with suspicion, if not open dislike. Even where the explanation of the possibilities for systematic survey work proves fruitless, the student will find that he has learned a great deal about the people he is studying.

Timing is an important factor in planning survey research in the developing nation. The student generally has no more than a year, and sometimes less. Furthermore, the political scene in the new nation is itself often changing rapidly and unpredictably. In Morocco the author knew that there were serious tensions within the party, and that once the party split there would be little chance of getting both factions to accept a similar inquiry. It is best that the student arrive with a questionnaire prepared and adjust this schedule to local conditions as well as his own limitations. Thus, in the Moroccan case the author felt pressed because of the internal strains in the Istiqlal, and agreed to send out the questionnaire before he was certain of how much cooperation he would get from the party on other matters. This meant that a good deal of the information sought in the organizational section of the questionnaire was later duplicated in personal interviews with local officials. After the questionnaire was at the printer's, the party agreed to give the author a sufficiently free hand in collecting organizational data. Information was collected in more reliable form from party records, documents and interviews with higher level officials. However, if the author had waited until he was sure of getting the party data he needed, he would very likely have run into more serious tension at party headquarters. There are no universal rules, but it seems wise to allow a month or two to develop local familiarity before proceeding with a survey. Since most students have an area interest to supplement their more systematic inquiry the time is not wasted.

Another problem that may go unforseen is printing the questionnaire. Printing facilities are very limited in most new nations. The author had not allowed for this expense in his budget, but found that the party press was willing to share costs. Nevertheless, printing had to be fitted in around the publication of

169

a daily newspaper and other more pressing party jobs. There was also a series of problems in typesetting and proof-reading. Although conditions no doubt vary greatly from country to country, the Moroccan linotypists were not accurate and did not understand the importance of careful layout. It was only after some insistence that they included lines for responses and spacing for ease of reading. As is indicated in Appendix I there were still some errors after careful proofing.

Every questionnaire involves a considerable amount of clerical work. The questionnaires had to be addressed and sorted out with envelopes. Bundles were made for each inspector to take to his region. New nations are remarkably short on skilled secretarial labor, most of which is absorbed by the government. This means that part-time help is scarce, and that persons of superior occupational status are reluctant to demean themselves by performing routine labor. There were no persons at party headquarters capable of making the clerical preparation. The result was that the author and his wife did most of the clerical work. The few times that a messenger boy or unskilled party worker was asked to do anything ended in disaster. At the time this questionnaire was administered there were very few Moroccan students interested in contemporary social science. As time passes there will undoubtedly be more interest in the techniques and problems of systematic sociology and political science. Some countries have established research organizations where help might be found.

Depending on the delicacy of the survey the student will encounter various problems of collection. The author was never certain, of course, but that the party would split in the midst of the study or that lower officials might obstruct the study. Nearly two months were required for the circulation of the questionnaires. One came from a secretary south of Ouarzazate who apologized for the slow communications by explaining that all reports were sent by camel. The agreement was that the questionnaires would be sealed in the supplied envelope and sent back to party headquarters via the inspector. This seems to have worked quite well in the regions where the inspector took an interest in the survey. All things considered, the response by party inspectorate (roughly a province) was either fairly large or it was not forthcoming at all. There was also some minor, but very alarming, misunderstanding over the circumstances under which the questionnaires were to be given to the author when they arrived at party headquarters. The more explicit the arrangements can be, the better.

The next step was translation. Again the local circumstances vary widely, but the author was able to procure the assistance of a minor official. Hand written Arabic is often extremely difficult to read and most students will undoubtedly need some help. The attitude toward the translation and preliminary evaluation of the data was very different from the attitude toward the preparations. The latter was clearly secretarial, and officials were not interested in the petty details. However, interest was aroused when the results began to be appearing in crude form. The official working with the author took great

170

interest and occasional delight in the rather tedious task. There were distinct advantages in having a person intimately familiar with the party and its local officials present during the translations. As has been noted some of the returns were too incomplete to be useful, and adjustments were made during translation and coding. Some time might have been saved if there was provision for coding on the questionnaire.

Since the Istiqlal survey there have been important additions to our fund of data, much of it available at the survey facilities of the University of Michigan, Williams College, and, more recently, the Center of International Studies of M.I.T. Some governmental data is also released from time to time, most notably the data used in Lerner's *The Passing of Traditional Society*. In preparing for similar studies in developing countries, the student would, of course, be well-advised to exploit existing resources and will generally find those involved in present efforts cooperative.